C0-ARK-341

PROPERTY OF

The
SOCIO-BEHAVIORAL APPROACH
and
APPLICATIONS TO SOCIAL WORK

Edited by
EDWIN J. THOMAS

With Papers Contributed by:

Robert D. Vinter
Richard B. Stuart
Sheldon D. Rose
Roger M. Lind
Edwin J. Thomas

Phillip Fellin
Jack Rothman
Henry J. Meyer
Rosemary C. Sarri

Mary E. Burns, *Recorder*

COUNCIL ON SOCIAL WORK EDUCATION
345 East 46th St.   New York, N.Y. 10017

HV
689
.T5

Copyright © 1967
by the
Council on Social Work Education, Inc.
Library of Congress Catalog Number 66, 25684

Printed in the United States of America by
Sowers Printing Co., Lebanon, Pennsylvania, 1967

FOREWORD

THE COUNCIL ON SOCIAL WORK EDUCATION included in its 1967 Annual Program Meeting a full-day colloquium on contemporary socio-behavioral theory and its application to social work education and practice.

This volume includes the six major papers presented by faculty members of The University of Michigan School of Social Work at the colloquium as well as the ensuing discussion between audience and speakers. Participants discussed, from their respective vantage points, how individuals, families, committees, peer groups, agencies, associations, neighborhoods, institutions, and communities become involved in behavioral modification or stabilization and specified the behaviorally relevant activities in each case.

The Council on Social Work Education takes great pleasure in presenting this volume. Few sessions at Annual Program Meetings of recent years have evoked so many comments and such spirited debate from so many quarters. We hope the point of view set forth in this book will lead practitioners and teachers to critically reexamine their own theoretical assumptions and the practice implications drawn from them. We anticipate that some readers will agree with the views expressed and others will differ; many will be helped by the insights presented and many will be troubled, but all will be challenged.

Appreciation is expressed to the faculty of the School of Social Work of The University of Michigan for their leadership in planning the colloquium and for their contributions, and to Dr. Edwin J. Thomas for editing the papers for publication.

ARNULF M. PINS
Executive Director

October, 1967

iii

PREFACE

AT THE 1967 ANNUAL PROGRAM of the Council on Social Work Education, a Faculty Colloquium was focused on a single topic: socio-behaviorial theory and its applications to social work practice. Limited time at the Colloquium did not permit presentation of the complete statements. This volume presents the series of papers delivered there and the ensuing discussion between speakers and members of the audience.

Three types of statements are contained here. The first is an exposition of the nature of socio-behavioral theory and its relevance to social work; the second consists of applications of this approach to practice in casework, group work, community organization, and administration; and the third is an exploration of the organizational requisites for a socio-behavioral technology. The major aim of these statements is not to propound a new intervention credo, but to examine the promise of the socio-behavioral approach for enhancing social work practice. Attention is directed to the application of an emerging domain of knowledge to traditional areas of service and to familiar problems of the field. The volume represents another example of necessary inquiry as professions seek to incorporate relevant, new knowledge for social uses.

The authors have not attempted to present a summary review of the underlying substance that constitutes the components of socio-behavioral knowledge or to detail the means by which it is being developed. These are tasks beyond the limits of this volume. Nevertheless, readers will necessarily gain a sense of the scope, boundaries, and sources of this knowledge. It is obvious that the knowledge being drawn upon is in no way restricted to that generated by behaviorists or derived from learning theory. The authors deliberately incorporate theoretical and empirical propositions from a wide range of social science areas, including role theory, small group and interaction processes, and organizational and community analyses. Moreover, they draw upon portions of known practice and intervention perspectives. In a very real sense, therefore, this approach depends and builds upon the existing resources of social work knowledge and practice.

But the approach is not indiscriminately eclectic. Thomas' paper outlines rigorous criteria for the selection and derivation of knowledge, and suggests some necessary procedures for its transformation. The socio-behavioral approach shares with more general viewpoints that emphasize the relevance of social science to social work a healthy respect for knowledge having empirical support. In addition, however, the socio-behavioral approach requires that the knowledge be directly relevant to the modification of behavior and that it afford concrete guidelines to direct helping activities. More than anything else, the socio-behavioral approach at present is perhaps best characterized as a framework within which knowledge from diverse sources can be selected, unified, and effectively harnessed to crucial professional processes.

We were fortunate to have had the foresight to record the questions and responses that followed each paper, for many significant issues were taken up. The relationship of this approach to others, to prevailing perspectives, and to ethical matters are among the topics embraced in the dialogue. Many of these questions, interestingly enough, are very much like those that tend to be raised in connection with the introduction of any viable body of knowledge or social practice. The reader will recall that questions such as these were raised when psychoanalytic theory emerged on the scene and, later, when the behavioral science revolution began to infuse social work. The answers to these important questions actually determine in part the eventual fate of any approach in the market place of professional knowledge and practice.

The volume also illuminates a matter of importance to the profession and especially to educators: namely, the role of faculty members in contributing to advances in social work knowledge and practice. The graduate professional school has long shared a responsibility to offer such contributions to the field. There is a variety of ways by which this responsibility can be served, and these papers embody several of them. Faculty persons are well situated to keep in touch with knowledge developments continuously occurring among the various social sciences and related disciplines. They are able to reconnoiter these developments, to codify potentially relevant knowledge, and to assist in its transformation for use by practitioners. Keeping in close touch with directions and requirements emerging from service agencies, faculty persons can also discern promising advances in technical proficiency which are initiated by practitioners. By fostering exchanges between these two major sources of innovation, faculty can heighten the benefits of each. The papers in this volume are the products of review in a defined area of inquiry, of derivation of intervention prescriptions for social work practice, and of preliminary field testing of some of these procedures. Validation and assimilation of such knowledge requires its communication through publication and teaching, critical response from practitioners, field demonstrations, and further testing.

The reflective reader of this volume may wonder whether it espouses a new "school of thought," or reveals one professional school's commitment to a new dogmatism. Although all of the authors are faculty members at the same school of social work, no two of them are mainly active in the same curriculum areas, nor do they share identical intellectual orientations and commitments. Indeed, the papers demonstrate that the professors' different curricular locations and theoretical perspectives have been major bases for contributions to a topic of common concern. Interest in the socio-behavioral approach is one juncture between the divergent theoretical pursuits of these particular individuals. An inquiry that crosscuts conventional instructional divisions provided, without reliance on committees, a promising opportunity for colleagial association. Apart from this volume—or from particular joint efforts some of them may undertake—the benefits of such collaboration will be diffused through their individual roles as teachers, researchers, or agency consultants. This is as it should be among professional schools that value intellectual diversity, that seek liberating modes of integration, and that eschew ideological dogmatism.

Since this approach builds upon existing knowledge from several sources, it represents no attempt to supplant other proven practices. In the short run at one or another school, the socio-behavioral approach will afford increments in the teaching by instructors of various intervention method or human behavior courses. In the long run, it will assume its proper place in the eclectic professional curriculum which continuously incorporates knowledge from diverse sources.

The authors of these papers wish to acknowledge debts to those who have provided important assistance in this work. For the past four years, agency field instructors have participated with faculty in special institutes focused on socio-behavioral knowledge and its practice applications. Their accomplishments have been partially summarized in an earlier publication[1] and have directly informed these papers. Students in a broad range of courses at both master's and doctoral levels have contributed through their critical response to this content, and through their exploratory use of it in field situations. Several field agencies, particularly Detroit's Neighborhood Service Organization, have provided opportunities for testing and application through faculty consultation, field demonstrations, and the like.

The University of Michigan School of Social Work and Dean Fedele F. Fauri have generously provided staff assistance and encouragement for this as well as for other lines of faculty endeavor. The warm interest of Marguerite Pohek of the C.S.W.E. and of Norman Roth and his Program Com-

---

[1] Edwin J. Thomas and Esther Goodman, eds., *Socio-behavioral Theory and Interpersonal Helping in Social Work: Lectures and Institute Proceedings* (Ann Arbor: Campus Publishers, 1965).

mittee for Faculty Conference Day provided the stimulus for the preparation, delivery, and eventual publication of these papers. We wish to acknowledge the good offices of the C.S.W.E. for helping in so many other ways to bring this publication into being. Dr. Arnulf M. Pins and Miss Karon Kehoe deserve special thanks for their help. The contributions of the Faculty Colloquium participants are included in the volume and are greatly appreciated. Among the various secretaries who helped prepare the manuscripts for this volume, we wish especially to acknowledge the competent assistance of Miss Lynn Nilles. Finally, the authors acknowledge their special debt to Edwin J. Thomas, whose intellectual leadership has been a moving force in this work, and whose colleagial guidance brought both the Colloquium and this volume into being.

Robert D. Vinter, Associate Dean
School of Social Work
University of Michigan

CONTRIBUTORS

All contributors are faculty members of The University of Michigan School of Social Work.

Mary E. Burns, M.S.W., Ph.D., Professor of Social Work

Phillip A. Fellin, M.S.W., Ph.D., Associate Professor of Social Work

Roger M. Lind, M.S.W., Ph.D., Professor of Social Work

Henry J. Meyer, M.A., Ph.D., Professor of Social Work, and of Sociology, College of Literature, Science, and the Arts

Sheldon D. Rose, M.S.W., M.S.S.W., Ph.D., Associate Professor of Social Work

Jack Rothman, M.S.W., Ph.D., Professor of Social Work

Rosemary C. Sarri, M.S.W., Ph.D., Professor of Social Work

Richard B. Stuart, M.S., D.S.W., Associate Professor of Social Work

Edwin J. Thomas, M.S.W., Ph.D., Professor of Social Work, and of Psychology, College of Literature, Science, and the Arts

Robert D. Vinter, M.S., Ph.D., Professor of Social Work and Associate Dean of the School of Social Work

CONTENTS

* *Mary E. Burns was recorder for all discussion material.*

I.
THE SOCIO-BEHAVIORAL APPROACH: ILLUSTRATIONS AND ANALYSIS

Edwin J. Thomas

Social Work is a relatively new profession that has grown and matured remarkably during its brief history. Its objectives have become increasingly well formulated, and it has made great progress in establishing its legitimacy as one of the professions dedicated to the improvement of human welfare. These, and other achievements, are especially noteworthy when one realizes that social work has labored to create its place in the division of professional endeavor during times of unusually rapid social change. The entire social surround—the technology, knowledge, and values—has been in flux during precisely the same period that the profession has been attempting to evolve its specialized competencies. Because of the significance of these changes for the knowledge, practices, and institutional forms of social work, the maturity of the profession depends as much upon how it adapts to new developments as it does upon the consolidation of its past and current endeavors.

There are at least two developments that are especially important in the current evolution of the socio-behavioral approach. The first is the production in recent years of an enormous body of information about individual and social change in the diverse specialties of the behavioral sciences and in selected quarters of the helping professions. Because this information has not yet been fully attended to and assimilated in the helping professions, there is now, for many of us, a large and rich backlog awaiting our perusal. This knowledge and practice, when carefully examined, promises to make significant contributions to the activities of professional helping that directly involve behavioral stabilization and change in individuals, groups, or larger aggregates. Specifically, such information promises to contribute to a social practice that is more firmly based upon empirically supported knowledge,

1

that affords more concrete, determinate action, and that allows for action having more demonstrable effectiveness. Although these are ambitious promises, every practitioner would probably agree that they are desirable. Most practitioners would also concur that current practice more often falls short of these ideal characteristics than reflects them.

The second development of importance in this context is an emerging awareness in social work and in related helping professions that the achievement of individual and social change is the central activity of professional helping. It cannot be denied that much of what is called "treatment" in work with individuals and groups turns out, when fully defined, to consist of specific behavior that is to be modified or maintained. Likewise, much of what is called "decision-making" and "action" when working with organizations and communities is revealed concretely to be the change or maintenance of given behavior by particular individuals, groups, or larger aggregates. The achievement of behavioral modification or stabilization is an identifiable objective of social work practice at all levels of intervention; and the stabilization or change in question may implicate single individuals, families, committees, or peer groups, as well as some or all of the members of larger aggregates such as agencies, associations, neighborhoods, institutions, and communities.

In asserting that behavioral maintenance or change is ultimately a central outcome of practice at all levels of intervention, the intention is not to obscure important differences between and among practices at various levels of intervention. Thus, when working with groups or large aggregates, it may be useful or even essential to conceptualize the objectives of change in terms of variables at the group, organizational, or community levels and to engage in intervention activities designed to change precisely these variables. Furthermore, the substantive knowledge of change and the details of the practice method will differ from one level of intervention to another.

Mention is made of these two particular developments because they are among those that strongly suggest a relatively distinct type of knowledge and practice useful to social work. This type of knowledge and practice is identified as the socio-behavioral approach. More important than the name, however, are the essential characteristics of the approach and their relation to the possibilities for increasing the effectiveness of efforts to achieve the change and stabilization of individuals and social systems. Not everything in this approach is new, of course, but there is enough that is distinctive, if not unique, to merit its isolation and conceptualization.

The objective of this initial statement is to formulate what now appear to be the requisites of this type of knowledge and practice as these apply to problems of maintaining and changing behavior of individuals and social systems. The specific substantive knowledge (such as the psychological, social psychological, or sociological propositions about change) that is illustrative

2

of socio-behavioral knowledge at various levels of intervention is not developed here, nor are the concrete actions in practice that illustrate socio-behavioral practice with individuals, groups, organizations, or communities. As the socio-behavioral approach matures, however, there will necessarily have to be an explication of the particular substantive knowledge and concrete practices distinctive for every level of intervention.

The requisites of socio-behavioral knowledge and practice are really just now becoming apparent. As more attention is given to the specific knowledge and practice identified as socio-behavioral at all levels of human aggregation, the criteria proposed here are very likely to be refined and extended.

This paper will employ illustrative studies to describe the nature of socio-behavioral knowledge as that body of empirical generalizations that is addressed to the change and stabilization of human behavior and that directs helpers toward determinate, concrete actions in practice. The practice of socio-behavioral theory will be discussed as consisting of the implementation of such knowledge for problems involving the change and stabilization of human behavior and of the behavioral specification of the relevant activities of the helper. In the papers to follow, the authors will discuss selected applications to various methods of social work (casework, group work, administration, and community organization) and some of the organizational requisites for a socio-behavioral technology.

FOUR EXAMPLES

Before discussing the distinguishing characteristics of socio-behavioral theory, four examples will be presented. Individual, group, organizational, and communal means to alter aspects of individual behavior are illustrated in these cases.[1] Furthermore, each "case" illustrates research that contributes to socio-behavioral knowledge and practice that, to some extent, is prototypic. However, the case studies are not all ideal examples of the socio-behavioral approach, since some are much more exemplary than others.

Tantrums and Extinction

The first case involves a twenty-one-month-old-boy who engaged in tyrannical tantrum behavior.[2] The child would scream and fuss when put to bed,

---

[1] These examples are not meant to be exemplars of the socio-behavioral approach at all levels of intervention, especially at the organizational and community levels.

[2] Carl D. Williams, "The Elimination of Tantrum Behavior By Extinction Procedures, *Journal of Abnormal and Social Psychology,* Vol. 59, No. 2 (September 1959) p. 269.

and his parents couldn't leave the bedroom until he was asleep. The parents generally spent one-half to two hours simply waiting in the room until the boy went to sleep.

After it was determined that the tantrum behavior was sustained by the attention provided by the parents at bedtime, it was decided to institute a regimen of extinction. The treatment program was based upon research indicating that by steadfastly withholding reinforcers that sustain the behavior, there will eventually be a diminution of the behavior in question. It was decided to put the child to bed in a leisurely and relaxed fashion. Then, following the usual pleasantries, the parent was to leave and the door to be left closed. On the first night, the child screamed for forty-five minutes; on the second, he did not fuss at all; on the third, he screamed for ten minutes; on the fourth, for six; on the fifth, for three; on the sixth, for two; and, finally, after seven sessions, there was no screaming at all. In a follow-up, there were no side- or after-effects, and the child was found to be friendly, expressive, and outgoing.

Delinquency Reduction and Groups

The second case illustrates the use of the group as a means to alter many aspects of the behavior of delinquent boys. The case derives from the Essexfields Demonstration Project in which a group rehabilitation center was established to work with sixteen- and seventeen-year-old delinquent boys.[3] Intake was restricted to delinquents called the "gang type"; "lone wolf" types and those who were severely disturbed, homosexual, or who had had previous institutional experience were excluded.

The group consisted of twenty boys who met every day from 7:30 a.m. to 10:00 p.m., and who returned to their homes each evening. After arriving at the rehabilitation center, each boy worked on a productive job for which he received $1.00 per day. In addition to working together, the boys ate lunch and supper as a group, traveled jointly to and from the place of work, and engaged in recreation for two and one-half hours a day. In the evenings, following supper, there was a period of one hour and half of group interaction guided by two trained therapists.

Because all of these boys were members of delinquent groups in the community, the objective of the project was to establish a social system in the rehabilitation center that would neutralize the effect of gang membership and, eventually, serve as a principal controlling force in the boys' lives. The boys and their therapists constituted a relatively self-contained social unit

---

[3] Saul Pilnick, Albert Elias, and Neal W. Clapp, "The Essexfields Concept: A New Approach to the Social Treatment of Juvenile Delinquents," *The Journal of Applied Behavioral Science,* Vol 2, No. 1 (Winter, 1966), pp. 109-124.

having its own norms, traditions, language, and conceptions of deviance. In each group there were always more "old" than "new" boys; the number of "old" boys employed to "seed" groups was at least ten and often fifteen. This partly assured the hegemony of prosocial rather than antisocial group forces. In addition, strong social pressures were placed upon the boys to adopt more conventional definitions of delinquency in place of gang definitions, and provision was made for much more freedom of choice concerning the boys' career alternatives. Throughout the project there was leader guidance, especially in the group sessions employed to support prosocial rather than antisocial norms. The objective was clearly to transfer loyalty from the old gang to the new group.

In this new social system, desired behavior was defined as engaging in productive work, "telling one's story" about why one became delinquent, accepting a more conventional definition of deviance than that provided by the gang, acknowledging the group's new conception of the factors that led to the deviancy in the first place, and working to overcome one's problems.

The norms in this social system emphasized "going deep," by which was meant that one should try to understand the true roots of one's problem; not "cliquing," by which was meant that one should not withhold relevant information from the group, either singly or by banding together with others; not "playing a role," by which was meant that one should not try to hide one's true feelings; and allowing oneself to be helped.

The norms described above were sanctioned in many ways. "Checking" really involved a method by which boys monitored the behavior of their fellows. "Hours" were simply forms of work meted out as punishment for deviations from the norms. Being "on report" consisted of a loss of a day's pay. Being "kept back" consisted of not being allowed to go with the group to the place of work. The ultimate sanction for failure consisted of being returned to the court.

Following release from the program, boys were returned to school, helped to get jobs, or both. Preliminary evaluation of the results revealed that of 246 boys entered in the program, 20 percent were found unsuitable. Of the remaining 196 who successfully completed the program, only 12 percent were committed to correctional institutions after release. This rough indication of recidivism contrasts favorably with the general rates, which are reported to range from 50 to 75 percent. Research on the evaluation of the outcome of the project is still in progress and control groups are being established for purposes of comparison.

The Token Economy

Moving now from the group to the organizational level, let us examine the token economy as one means by which a residential institution can alter the behavior of its members.[4] In this "case" study, one ward of a mental hospital containing 45 female mental patients was set aside for purposes of demonstration and research. Some or all of these patients were participants in a series of related studies.

All relevant activities in the ward were controlled to examine the effects of reinforcements, mediated by tokens, upon the jobs performed by patients. Six types of reinforcer made available fell into the following categories: privacy (such as selection of a room, a personal chair); leave from the ward (such as a twenty-minute walk on hospital grounds); social interaction with staff (such as a private audience with a social worker); devotional opportunities; recreational opportunities; and commissary items (such as candy, coffee, sandwich, toilet articles). Token values by which these could be obtained were established. For example, a patient could obtain a private audience with the ward psychologist with twenty tokens and a private audience with the social worker with one hundred tokens. The latter, incidentally, was about the most expensive item of all! Tokens could be exchanged for reinforcers three times a day.

In one set of experiments, a token economy was established for the performance of off-ward jobs (e.g., dietary, clerical, laboratory, or laundry work). In exchange for six hours of daily performance of any one of these jobs, 70 tokens were paid. It was found that performance on preferred as well as nonpreferred jobs was controlled entirely by the reinforcers dispensed. That is, patients would perform a nonpreferred job for tokens, and do so consistently for six hours a day, in preference to working on a preferred job without payment in tokens. Furthermore, when tokens were dispensed prior to completion of the work patients simply stopped working.

In another inquiry, the effectiveness of tokens in controlling performance of work involving on-ward jobs was examined. It was found that performance on such jobs as dietary assistant, waitress, sales clerk assistant, secretarial assistant, ward-cleaning assistant, assistant janitor, and self-care activities was almost completely controlled by the token reinforcers: when reinforcement was made contingent upon performance on these jobs, there was a high degree of successful performance, and when reinforcement was not contingent upon performance, performance dropped off radically.

In still another study in this series, information was provided concerning the effectiveness of the tokens in the choice of jobs. When patients were given a choice between nonpreferred jobs reinforced by tokens and preferred jobs in which there were incidental, extraneous social reinforcements without the provision of tokens, it was found that the patients chose jobs paying tokens.

Altogether, these experiments reveal that patients can be aided to per-

---

[4] Teodoro Ayllon and Nicholas H. Azrin, "The Measurement and Reinforcement of Behavior of Psychotics," *Journal of the Experimental Analysis of Behavior,* Vol. 8, No. 6 (November 1965), pp. 357-385.

form independently and effectively in the ways indicated. Although performance of diverse hospital jobs is pertinent for most patients in terms of increasing aspects of their social effectiveness, it is clear from these studies that token economies may be applied as well to behavior that more obviously relates to therapeutic objectives, as, for example, using tokens to strengthen role behavior outside of the institution. Experiments along these and other lines are currently in progress in other institutions.[5]

Civil Resocialization

The last case study to be discussed illustrates the use of a "transitional community" to change the attitudes and behavior of prisoners of war being repatriated into civilian roles.[6] The experiment in question was undertaken in Britain in 1945, when large numbers of British prisoners of war had to be repatriated. Civil Resettlement Units were established in diverse localities in the country. Altogether, some 40,000 to 50,000 volunteers were involved. The men entered units closest to their homes, each unit containing some 240 men.

The problem of the former POW being repatriated into civil life was analyzed as one involving "desocialization." This was viewed as consisting of failure to take proper social roles, to sustain social relationships, and most importantly, to assimilate the culture of one's social surrounding.

Men voluntarily entered the Resettlement Units for periods of four to five weeks, but this was extended to three months, if necessary. Activities in the Resettlement Units were ordered in phases, as follows: reception, settling in, orientation, and planning. At reception, which lasted three days, the man joined a section of 15 members, the section being one of four in a syndicate. Discipline was carried out mainly by group means, and there was rotating membership in all the groups so that at all times the tradition characteristic of the unit was dominant. During this initial period the men made friends. Then, during the first week, the men attended workshops, received information, had discussions, and were allowed to attend dances. During the second week there were voluntary visits to factories, shops, and training centers. During the third and fourth weeks, there were more individual assignments: activities relating to employment were rehearsed, and personal problems involving employment and the family were discussed with the repatriate and members of his family.

---

[5] *Ibid.*, p. 382.

[6] A. T. M. Wilson, E. L. Trist, and Adam Curle, "Transitional Communities and Social Reconnection: A Study of the Civil Resettlement of British Prisoners of War," in Guy E. Swanson, Theodore M. Newcomb, and Eugene L. Hartley, *Readings In Social Psychology,* Revised Edition (New York: Henry Holt and Company, 1952), pp. 561-582.

A limited follow-up study of this social experiment was undertaken in which it was found that men repatriated through the Resettlement Units displayed much more normative and supernormative behavior and less subnormative behavior than former POW's who did not elect to participate in such resocialization.

Compared with the other examples given, this example has some limitations, which will be pointed out shortly. This type of transitional resocialization, nonetheless, is, to some extent, prototypic of that carried out by many contemporary transitional agencies.

REQUISITES OF SOCIO-BEHAVIORAL KNOWLEDGE

With the above examples in mind, some of the main requisites of socio-behavioral knowledge will now be considered. Common to all of the examples discussed are at least three significant characteristics that distinguish socio-behavioral knowledge from other types.

Relevance to Behavioral Maintenance and Change

Socio-behavioral knowledge is that which pertains directly to the maintenance or change of behavior. Problems of change can be specified more precisely as involving either the acquisition, strengthening, weakening, or elimination of behavior. Problems of maintenance involve sustaining behavior at a given level. The words "behavioral control" or, simply, "control" may be used to cover all of these phenomena. When behavioral control is spoken of as the domain of inquiry for socio-behavioral knowledge, it is done so in the ethically neutral sense. No implication of coercion or improper manipulation by others is intended.

The diverse features of behavioral maintenance and change have all been illustrated in the examples. In the extinction of tantrums, the task was to eliminate the fussing and screaming when going to bed. In the Essexfields demonstration, one of the objectives was to eliminate delinquent behavior, another, to reduce the control of the neighborhood gang. The establishment of behavior was also illustrated in this case. Specifically, the therapists wished the delinquents to acquire proper habits associated with working, to acquire the behaviors associated with the role of the "helped person," and to increase prosocial behavioral options. Problems of acquisition and maintenance of behavior have been highlighted in the studies involving the token economy where there was an endeavor to establish and maintain performance on various hospital jobs. In the British Civil Resettlement Units, one of the objectives was to reinstate dormant and little-used features of a prosocial role repertoire associated with diverse activities of civilian life.

8

Empirical Support

A related and equally significant feature of socio-behavioral knowledge is its empirical corroboration. The results of scientific research, evaluative studies and demonstrations, as well as of documented practical experience and naturalistic observation, may all serve to provide necessary empirical corroboration of knowledge. Although not all knowledge about behavioral maintenance and change will necessarily possess the same scientific pedigree, it is clear that the more the empirical support for the knowledge, the more confidence may be had in its validity.

There is strong experimental support for the phenomenon of extinction, the procedure employed to eliminate the tantrum behavior. Likewise, the principles of reinforcement as employed in the token economies have been extensively studied. There is also corroboration from diverse sources for the potency of social systems in altering behavior. It was this knowledge that was basic to the Essexfields experiment. The large-scale experiment in social reconnection that employed Civil Resettlement Units as transitional social systems drew implicitly upon knowledge of continuities in role training, resocialization, and group and community systems to achieve changes. However, the nature of the knowledge and the status of its empirical support are least clearly apparent in this study as compared with the other three. But in each of the case studies selected, at least some empirically corroborated knowledge was found being implemented. And furthermore, each of the studies is a research contribution in its own right.

Operationality in Action

A third and essential characteristic of socio-behavioral knowledge is its potentiality for affording concrete, determinate action. Such knowledge is referred to as being operational knowledge. There are two sets of criteria that, in the author's view, make knowledge operational.[7] Both sets of criteria pertain to the referents of the knowledge in question.

One set of criteria of operational knowledge pertains to its "engineerability." By this we mean that the indicators, in the world, that make the concepts of the knowledge operational, have the following characteristics: they are identifiable, accessible, and manipulatable. Consider reinforcement as an example of a concept whose referents have engineerability. In the token economies, in which knowledge of reinforcement as it relates to operant behavior was implemented, a large number of reinforcing conditions was identi-

---

[7] For a more detailed discussion of these "referent criteria," the reader is referred to Edwin J. Thomas, "Selecting Knowledge from Behavioral Science," in *Building Social Work Knowledge: Report of a Conference* (New York: National Association of Social Workers, 1964), pp. 38-48.

fied. These conditions were all activities already accessible, to varying degrees, in the lives of the patients in the hospital. The reinforcing conditions were manipulated in the experiments by simply making them contingent upon the performance of hospital jobs.

A second set of criteria defining operationality becomes pertinent after the engineerability of the referents has been established. These concern the "practicality" of the operations. Practicality is defined by three distinct factors: the potency of the indicators when manipulated, the ethical suitability of such manipulations, and the economy of their operation. Although all of the operations in the studies described possess practicality, as conceived here, for purposes of illustration consider again the study involving tantrums. The potency of the operation of eliminating the reinforcement for the tantrum behavior was clearly indicated by the rapidity with which the tantrum behavior diminished under extinction. The ethical suitability of the procedure consisted of obtaining the parents' permission and cooperation to withhold the reinforcing events that previously sustained the tantrum behavior. Furthermore, because the child had been under supervision for medical problems for most of the early months of his life, the physician's permission to engage in the extinction regimen was obtained. The ethical impunity of the extinction regimen was further affirmed by experimental and clinical knowledge that this procedure is not likely to have any long term or adverse side effects.[8] The economy of withholding reinforcement for tantrum behavior deserves little comment, for there are few activities that are less costly in time and effort.

REQUISITES OF SOCIO-BEHAVIORAL PRACTICE

In contrast to knowledge, socio-behavioral practice consists of the characteristic activities of the helping person as he endeavors to achieve behavioral change or maintenance.

Implementation of Socio-Behavioral Knowledge

The first requisite of socio-behavioral practice is the implementation of socio-behavioral knowledge. Deliberate, planful implementation of socio-behavioral knowledge helps assure that the operations engaged in to achieve change involve the proper manipulation of variables. Consider the difference between a naive attempt to extinguish tantrums and a theoretically informed one. A naive parent might try to ignore his child's tantrums once or perhaps twice

---

[8] There may be a temporary increase of the behavior being extinguished at the beginning of the procedure and also some "emotional reactions," these generally being brief but sometimes strong.

and if the tantrums persist, as they probably would after so few attempts to extinguish them, the parent might give up and conclude that his technique was faulty. By "giving up," this parent would probably return to occasional reinforcement of the tantrums. The irony is that periodic reinforcement serves to sustain behavior very well rather than to eliminate it.[9] A theoretically informed parent, in contrast, would steadfastly withhold reinforcement for the tantrums until they were eliminated, and this might require many episodes of tantrums that were not reinforced.

The case studies cited differ significantly in terms of the implementation of socio-behavioral knowledge. Although it is explicit and clear that knowledge of extinction was employed in the case of tantrums, that principles of reinforcement were implemented in the token economy, and that social systems theory was used in the Essexfields experiment, the relationship between the change operations and the knowledge being employed in the British social reconnection experiment was much less clear and, at best, only implicit.

Behavioral Specification

It is becoming increasingly clear that one of the significant hallmarks of socio-behavioral practice is the behavioral specification of the relevant activities of achieving stabilization and change. There appear to be at least five important occasions for being behaviorally specific.

The first involves behavioral specification of the problematic behavior. Such specification consists of the overtly identifiable aspects of the behavior defined as problematic as well as the behaviors of those who judge the behavior as problematic. The responses themselves are generally those that occur in surfeit or deficit or are otherwise inappropriate (e.g., are insufficiently controlled by common reinforcers or discriminative stimuli). Such responses may be defined as problematic by the person himself, by the professional helper, or by others. The behavior is itself not viewed as inherently psychopathological, deviant, or maladaptive. It is through social definition that all behavior comes to be construed as problematic or non-problematic. Thus, if the tantrums in the case example were not defined as problematic by the parents and the therapist, there would have been no basis for acting in the situation. In this view, tantrum behavior is not inherently psychopathological or deviant.

Of all the case studies presented here, the problematic behaviors were least well stipulated in the experiment involving social reconnection of former prisoners of war. However, despite their diversity and complexity, such behaviors are, in principle, amenable to detailed and accurate stipulation.

---

[9] Indeed, by trying to extinguish and then "giving up," our naive parent exacerbates the problem in perhaps the worst way.

A second occasion for being specific behaviorally concerns the identification of the controlling conditions for the problematic behavior. This does not necessarily imply any deep-seated hypothetical, underlying, maladaptive state. Rather, the emphasis is upon contemporaneous environmental conditions that, at least for individual behavior, either reinforce, elicit, or serve as discriminative cues for the problematic behaviors in question. In the case of the tantrum, the tantrum behavior was revealed to be controlled by the reinforcing properties of the attention and physical presence of the parents; in the case of the Essexfields project, the delinquent behavior was partly controlled by membership in a gang having deviant traditions and norms, combined with an effective sanctioning system; in the token economies, the failure to perform given jobs was discovered to be controlled in large measure by the reinforcing contingencies of the hospital; in the social reconnection experiment, the controlling conditions were apparently not examined in detail although it may be inferred that the deprivation of the POW experience itself was operative along with the disuse of civilian role skills and, in some cases, the now new social environment that many faced after the war.

A third occasion for behavioral specificity involves the exact indication of the desired behavior. Behaviors specified as desirable include not only the terminal behaviors, but also the range of intermediate behaviors. This entire set of behaviors, when ordered from initial through the intermediate to the terminal, constitutes a "behavioral curriculum." The analogy to an educational curriculum is apt, for it connotes the desirability of complete and ordered specification of all desired behaviors. In existing practice, intermediate and terminal behaviors are most often spoken of as treatment "goals." If there is a difference between the formulation of so-called treatment goals and a behavioral curriculum, it is that in the latter there is a greater degree of exact specification and a more complete ordering of desired behavior.

Behavioral curricula appear to occur in practice in at least two important forms. The "simple curriculum" consists of either problematic behavior ordered in terms of degree or desirable behavior ordered similarly. The behavioral curriculum implicit in the treatment of the child with tantrums involved no tantrum behavior as the desired terminal outcome, with progressively less and less of such behavior in the intermediate range. Increasing the amount of performance of the desired behavior is illustrated in the studies of the token economies in which performance for given periods of time was the desired terminal behavior, with decreasing amounts of performance indicating less of the desired behavior. When behaviors can be reckoned in terms of more or less of essentially the same thing, either when eliminating or establishing such behaviors, it is convenient to speak of a continuous, accretionary behavioral curriculum.

Another simple type of curriculum is the accretionary one in which there is a noncontinuous relationship between and among behaviors. For example, in one phase of the Essexfields demonstration there was an endeavor to work on various behaviors each of which was separate, but each of which was presumed to bear a sequential relationship to the others. Thus, in order for these boys to assume properly the role of the "helped person," it can be inferred that they first had to tell "their story," then to accept a new definition of their prior delinquent behavior, and finally to "work to overcome" the problems alleged to have generated the delinquent behavior.

The second important form is the "multiple curriculum." By this is meant simply a "problem" that consists of diverse behavioral curricula. One recalls that the Essexfields project enjoined the boys to engage in productive work, this being one set of behaviors that may be ordered into a curriculum; a second involved the behaviors just mentioned having to do with the "helped role" (telling one's story, etc.); and a third required differentiating diverse behavioral options to delinquency. Unfortunately, the curricula in the social reconnection experiment were not described. However, judging from the diversity and complexity of the entire program of services and the time when the experiment was done, it can be inferred that detailed curricula were not evolved for each man. If they were, such curricula would probably have been multiple; they would undoubtedly have been most variegated, with each man having his own combination.

When desired behaviors are identified and arranged properly into behavioral curricula, they enable the practitioner to negotiate a behaviorally specific contract with the client, and they provide for definition and structuring of the helping relationship so that the helper knows what to do next and what progress has been made.

The fourth occasion for being specific behaviorally concerns identification of the techniques employed to achieve behavioral modification. Ideally, these techniques should be operationally concrete as well as functionally specific. For example, if one wishes to establish a token economy, it is not enough to provide tokens for engaging in certain performances; it is also necessary to have the tokens serve as exchange, in properly calculated amounts, for activities varying in their reinforcing properties for the individuals in question.

The techniques of socio-behavioral practice are currently being isolated, conceptualized, and studied. The "simpler" socio-behavioral techniques presently appear to involve two types of basic operations. The first is that of presenting a stimulus. This is illustrated in the experiments with the token economies in which performance was reinforced with the dispensing of tokens that could be exchanged for reinforcing activities. The other operation involves the termination or postponement of a stimulus. One particular variant of this was illustrated in the study of tantrums in which the procedure consisted of withholding reinforcement when problematic behavior was emitted, resulting eventually in the complete diminution of the problematic behavior in question. Operations of the sort discussed may occur contingently or non-

13

contingently in relation to given responses. Considering the many possible variations of operations and their contingence with respect to given responses, one may define not only the simple techniques of extinction and positive reinforcement, as indicated above, but also negative reinforcement and punishment. [10]

The "complex" techniques, in contrast, generally involve more than one simple technique. However, despite their complexity, such techniques are potentially as specifiable as the simpler ones. Thus, given adequate information, the behaviorally operative factors created in the social system in the Essexfields demonstration could be identified. In addition to the use of extinction, positive and negative reinforcement, and punishment, in diverse combinations, it can be inferred from the description of that project that most relevant aspects of the entire group situation were structured. The group structuring apparently consisted of designation of particular group functions, goals, and structure and this structure was importantly related to the roles defined for the members. Indeed, since the roles of the members were themselves structured by examining them, specific features of a sanctioning system, a prescriptive system, and a performance system can be identified. On the basis of present information, it would appear that "group structuring," as well as "role structuring," are emerging as identifiable complex techniques of change. Eventually, distinct types of complex techniques of change may be identified for organizations, communities, and perhaps even for societies. Other more common complex techniques of change currently being used in interpersonal helping include coaching, shaping, satiation, negative practice, behavioral rehearsal, differential reinforcement, verbal instructions, counterconditioning, and model presentation. "Role structuring" and "group structuring" may soon be specifiable as complex techniques, as may diverse features of "organizational structuring." [11]

The fifth occasion for being behaviorally specific involves the short- and long-term outcomes of change. There are two factors here of practical interest. One involves the extent to which the desired behaviors are actually achieved and the other involves the extent to which other beneficial or adverse changes occur. The empirical determination of the outcome of change is illustrated in all the studies cited as case examples. The direct monitoring of outcome is best illustrated in the ongoing records kept on behavior in the studies of extinction and the token economy. In contrast, the other two studies employed follow-up procedures not unlike those commonly employed in evalu-

---

[10] For an explication of such a systematic framework, see Arthur J. Bachrach, "Some Applications of Operant Conditioning to Behavior Therapy," in Joseph Wolpe, Andrew Salter, and Leo J. Reyna, eds., *The Conditioning Therapies: The Challenge in Psychotherapy* (New York: Holt, Rinehart and Winston, 1964), pp. 62-81, especially pp. 64-68.

[11] For exposition of some of the techniques, see, Edwin J. Thomas, "Selected Socio-behavioral Techniques and Principles," *Social Work,* in press.

ative research on the effectiveness of services. In practice, emphasis is placed upon the behavioral specification of the outcome, because such determination serves greatly to eliminate uncertainty about the effectiveness of the change endeavor. If the change effort is successful and there are no adverse side effects, the practitioner can certify to the accomplishment of the service objectives; and analogously, if the change efforts are ineffective, or if there are adverse concomitants, the practitioner has learned something about the techniques of his practice and the specific problems of the client that still require attention.

POSTSCRIPT

The principal justification for advocating a socio-behavioral approach is that it promises to be a more effective way to accomplish professional objectives relating to the achievement of behavioral change and stabilization. A surprisingly large amount of research on the effectiveness of various socio-behavioral techniques has already been conducted. Much of this has involved the behavioral therapies, but other socio-behavioral approaches have been examined as well. Although much more research is required, available evidence indicates that socio-behavioral approaches are more effective than more traditional approaches, or than inaction. Of course, the choice of technique must ultimately be decided by empirical evidence.

While we await more complete information, the socio-behavioral approach provides a viable and potentially durable framework within which to work. Contained within it are important empirical bases lacking in many more traditional approaches. One of these is the application of knowledge that is itself based upon empirical corroboration. The other is the use of concrete techniques in the context of a behaviorally specific practice that at least assures the practitioner that the degree of effectiveness of his efforts will be demonstrable. Knowing his specific successes and failures, he can then adapt his techniques accordingly and, more generally, contribute to the knowledge and practice of the approach within which he is working. A more thoroughly empirical social practice, which, in a way, is at the heart of the socio-behavioral approach, has the singular virtue of letting nature speak so that we can more clearly hear the call. In the long run, one cannot go far wrong if that call is heeded.

Discussion

Question 1. I wondered whether your concentration on behavior as a point of attack takes us back to a period of medicine when the physician was very concerned with the symptom of fever and spent all his time and effort in the elimination of fever rather than concerning himself with the factors that contributed to the fever, that is, going back to a more general appraisal of the individual's adaptation to his total situation. I know that the behavior is specifically defined, and I have no quarrel with that; but this seems to imply a less holistic concern for the individual's environment than a specific attack on the presenting behavior.

Thomas. That's a good question. Why attack the fever when there is an underlying disease? That is the heart of it, isn't it? (Affirmative nod from the questioner.)

In this approach, "behavior is behavior," to make a slogan of it. There is no underlying psychic disease, except that which can be organically demonstrated. There are no such things as "schizophrenic processes" or psychoneuroses, as psychic diseases. The medical metaphor is misleading and wrong unless the organic basis for problem behavior has been demonstrated. Without demonstrable organicity, there is only problematic behavior (e.g., indications of anxiety, strange thought processes, strange verbalizations—all defined by someone as problematic). When these problematic behaviors are altered in an ethically suitable way by members of a behavior-controlling environment, there is no evidence with which I am familiar to indicate that the so-called phenomenon of symptom substitution will occur. When you alter behavior and sustain the controlling conditions for that alteration, the new behavior will clearly tend to be maintained. Take the example of the tantrums. In this case, tantrums were eliminated by withholding the attention that sustained them in the first place. Or take bedwetting. You eliminate bedwetting and that's that. Now there may be some other problems, but that is another kettle of fish. Thus, if a child has tantrums *and* is anxious in the presence of others, these are two different problems until the search for controlling conditions reveals a clear-cut interrelationship. If the problems are unrelated. each is attacked in its own terms; if the problems are related to the same antecedents, a unified but behaviorally specific approach would be called for.

Question 2. In your use of the term socio-behavioral theory and your description of the concepts here, do you think that this is something distinct from learning theory approaches of such persons as Ullmann, Krasner, Eysenck, Wolpe, Bandura, and Walters?

Thomas. Yes, you question what is the difference between a socio-behavioral approach and behavior modification by behavioral therapy? An important feature of behavioral therapy is that there is reliance upon certain types of learning theory applied mainly, but not exclusively, in face-to-face contacts. We are concerned with a more general approach in which behavioral therapy and modification would be instances. These would be included but we would not wish to restrict ourselves exclusively to them. We are concerned with drawing upon knowledge from social systems and role theories that pertain to change. We are concerned with performance and motivation theory in psychology as well as with theories of organizations, socialization, and deviance. A general, empircally based, operational body of knowledge is what is being sought here.

Furthermore, we are not thinking merely of change contexts in which there is a face-to-face relationship. Although it is probably unfair to say that the behavioral modification people are exclusively so restricted, in social work we are often expressly concerned with much more than face-to-face relationships. We are concerned as well with altering family, organizational, and community contexts, to name a few others.

Question 3. Do you have any openings to incorporate other theoretical formulations with yours?

Thomas. The point of view expressed here involves a certain form of eclecticism as refined, focused, and guided by the criteria discussed. The socio-behavioral approach is concerned with knowledge about the change and stabilization of behavior. *Any* empirically based knowledge from *any* specialized discipline in the behavioral sciences or from *any* practice endeavor qualifies, providing that it meets the criteria discussed here. That's the intention.

Now, how do we handle personality theory or some of the other bodies of knowledge that are very important in our current base of knowledge? Remember, the focus in the socio-behavioral approach is exclusively upon knowledge addressed to change and stabilization of behavior. That means that if the knowledge from personality deals with the characteristics of individuals (such as self-esteem, authoritarianism, and intelligence) that have been demonstrated to relate to changeability, then that knowledge is of crucial importance. Knowledge of "natural" developmental changes would be relevant but somewhat less so for achieving change *per se,* and knowledge of hypothetical personality characteristics (e.g., the "ego") would be even less relevant to the task of behavioral modification. Analogously, in role theory there is a great deal that doesn't pertain directly to the change of behavior, but there are portions of role theory addressed to change (e.g., the

17

material on role playing). Role playing has been demonstrated to be an effective way of acquiring and maintaining behaviors, and we should make use of this information. The portions of knowledge in other bodies of information that do not pertain *directly* to behavioral change or maintenance are less useful to socio-behavioral theory, but perhaps they may be useful for other purposes in social work.

Question 4. I am concerned about the relevance of the different theories to social work purposes. I understand that the approach is related to questions of change and maintenance of the behavior, but I am wondering if there isn't an overriding purpose of social work. Also, I am wondering where does development fit into this. Is it subsumed under change, maintenance, or is it something that is excluded?

Thomas. You are asking first about the pertinence of this subject to social work. I would like to emphasize that in virtually everything we do in social work there is a change component. I am certain that if we examine specifically what we are doing, we will disclose that fundamentally in all areas of intervention in social work we are attempting to bring about the maintenance or alteration of behavior. I know that's a strong statement, but I believe firmly that it can be sustained. Socio-behavioral theory is the first approach in social work with which I am familiar which involves knowledge as well as practice addressed expressly to this core, fundamental activity of the profession. It is to me an embarrassing irony that the profession has adopted theory after theory which is only tangentially related to change.

How about the values of social work? Knowledge about everything can be used for good or ill. The knowledge of socio-behavioral theory is not a value system, although I am sure that the ethical philosophers could infer values contained therein. Our approach has been to respect the values of the profession. We wish to use this knowledge and form of practice to achieve modification and maintenance of behavior in behalf of the achievement of social work values.

Now the other part of your question had to do with the natural phases of development for individuals as they grow up. The most pertinent body of information for socio-behavioral theory, as was indicated, is that which pertains directly to planned change. "Natural" changes of persons are a kind of amalgam of unintended and intended changes of behavior and developmental sequences paced by biological factors. As such, this knowledge would generally not be as directly pertinent as information about behavioral modification.

II.
APPLICATIONS OF BEHAVIOR THEORY TO SOCIAL CASEWORK

Richard B. Stuart

As a scientifically based helping profession, social casework can fortify its practice with the adaptation of an empirically corroborated theory pertaining directly to the maintenance and change of behavior. Behavior theory is such an approach. It provides a clear series of practical links between the identification of client distress, the delineation of clinical goals, the formulation of plans of intervention, and the measurement of outcome. The material that follows will characterize the basic elements of behavioral theory relevant to casework in the areas of the structure of treatment, the nature of behavioral assessment, and the nature of intervention. A case will then be described to illustrate this approach.

STRUCTURE OF TREATMENT

There are three basic assumptions in a behavioral approach to casework. The first is that *all social behavior is learned and can be modified through the application of the principles of learning.*[1] The change process begins with a precise description of problem behavior and then leads to a planful alteration of the controlling conditions and contingencies of behavior. There are no mentalisms and internal mechanisms in the assessment and no hypothetical constructs in the logic of the plans of change. Furthermore, it is believed that there is no class of learned behaviors which cannot be altered through the application of learning principles.

---

[1] Leonard P. Ullmann and Leonard Krasner, "Introduction," in Leonard P. Ullmann and Leonard Krasner, eds., *Case Studies in Behavior Modification* (New York: Holt, Rinehart and Winston, 1965), pp. 1-63.

The second basic assumption of the behavioral approach is that *all psychotherapies involve a teaching-and-learning experience* for therapist and client respectively. To deny this is to deny the commonplace observation that the therapist rewards the client with attention and approval when adaptive efforts consistent with the therapists's guidance are manifest, or that attention and approval are withdrawn when the expected adaptive strivings are not present. In fact, it has been suggested that it is impossible for two people to interact without influencing (controlling) each other. An examination of this supposition recently demonstrated that despite strong beliefs in therapist neutrality, when Carl Rogers offered 85 nondirective interviews to a client, he differentially rewarded and increased the frequency of certain client behaviors through the selective application of empathy, acceptance and directiveness.[2]

If learning is inevitable in psychotherapy, the third assumption of behavior therapy is that *"a more deliberate application of our knowledge of the learning process to psychotherapy would yield far more effective results."*[3] Learning is used here in its broadest context, including the acquisition, maintenance, alteration, and elimination of behavior. While the direct application of laboratory principles to *in vivo* situations is not without hazards, much can be learned from laboratory and field studies of learning that can aid in the attainment of therapeutic objectives. Explicit application of these principles may increase therapeutic effectiveness[4] and provide the opportunity to forestall violations of therapeutic morality that arise when therapists influence patients without their own or their patients' acceptance of this fact.

GOAL DETERMINATION

All behavioral treatment is *goal oriented,* and nothing occurs during the therapeutic interchange that is not relevant to the attainment of goals. Society assumes the right to determine the behavioral change goals with certain categories of clients such as children, psychotics and offenders. While these clients may not participate in goal determination, it is essential that they become aware of the therapeutic goals as soon as practical. (It is recognized that the term "practical" suggests a broad range of variance, as determined in individual treatment situations.) With all other clients, a therapeutic *contract* is formed in which:

---

[2] Charles B. Truax, "Reinforcement and Nonreinforcement in Rogerian Psychotherapy," *Journal of Abnormal Psychology,* Vol. 71, No. 1 (February, 1966), pp. 1-9.

[3] Albert Bandura, "Psychotherapy as a Learning Process," *Psychological Bulletin,* Vol. 58, No. 2 (March, 1961), pp. 143-159.

[4] See for example: Hans J. Eysenck and Stanley Rachman, *The Causes and Cures of Neurosis* (San Diego: Robert S. Knapp, 1965).

. . . the therapist is the *agent of the patient,* and undertakes to treat only what is specifically determined jointly by the patient and therapist.[5] (Italics mine.)

Thus the goals are a product of mutual assent. They are explicit and they are amenable to periodic monitoring by both client and therapist. Mutuality assures commitment to goal attainment by the client and therapist. Explicitness creates the condition necessary for precise treatment planning. Finally, monitorability allows both the client and therapist to have immediate information about the effectiveness of their efforts so that adjustments in the plan are possible.

RELATIONSHIP

The therapist-client relationship is the matrix through which treatment is administered in behavioral treatment, as in all individual therapies. Two therapist tasks deserve mention in this connection. First, the therapist assumes directive responsibility throughout the treatment, and second, the outcome of treatment is the responsibility of the therapist. As Wolpe and Lazarus observe:

> Just as the unlearning of the experimental neurosis is completely in the control of the experimenter, so the overcoming of human neurosis is within the control of the therapist through techniques quite similar to those used in the laboratory.[6]

The therapist undertakes to aid the client in the formulation of his goals and then develops a treatment plan consistent with these goals. He explains the rationale for the plan so that this didactic component of treatment is as explicit as the goals and treatment plan. He then assumes responsibility for managing the highly structured therapeutic interchange in order to exclude material not pertinent to the attainment of goals or their modification.

The second task of the therapist is to increase the attractiveness of treatment for the client; that is, to increase the client's willingness to participate in the behavior change operation. Procedures used to achieve this goal include descriptions of probable outcomes and selective use of rewards. These and others are well described elsewhere.[7]

---

[5] Edward S. Sulzer, "Research Frontier: Reinforcement and the Therapeutic Contract," *Journal of Counseling Psychology,* Vol. 9, No. 3 (Fall, 1962), p. 271.

[6] Joseph Wolpe and Arnold A. Lazarus, *Behavior Therapy Techniques* (Oxford: Pergamon Press, 1960), p. 17.

[7] Arnold P. Goldstein, Kenneth Heller and Lee B. Sechrest, *Psychotherapy and the Psychology of Behavior Change* (New York: John Wiley, 1966), pp. 73-145.

ADAPTIVE VERSUS MALADAPTIVE BEHAVIOR

Behavior therapists accept the view that deviance is defined by the community with which the individual interacts. Adaptive behaviors must be compatible with community expectations and with the attainment of individual goals. Maladaptive behaviors are either incompatible with community expectations or individual goals, or both.

The behavior therapist is concerned with two aspects of behavior: its frequency and its controlling conditions. When the behavior of autistic children is studied,[8] it is seen that maladaptive behaviors, such as atavisms, occur at very high relative frequencies while adaptive behaviors, such as social responses, occur at correspondingly low frequencies. The behaviors of normal children, conversely, contain high frequencies of adaptive behaviors and low frequencies of maladaptive behaviors. A second feature that differentiates the repertoires of autistics and normals is the relative infrequency of socially mediated behaviors among the former group as opposed to the relative frequency of such behaviors in the latter group. Large segments of the behavioral repertoire of autistics is maintained by concrete reinforcers. Among normals, concrete reinforcers are important, but social reinforcers control large sectors of the repertoire. Increasing the frequency and range of socially mediated behaviors is one of the chief means by which the frequency of adaptive behaviors is increased. This process is enhanced by the fact that, in any individual, adaptive and maladaptive behaviors coexist.[9]

CONTROLLING CONDITIONS OF BEHAVIOR

From a behaviorist's point of view, all human behavior is a result of the individual's responses to internal and external stimuli. Behavior is said to be maladaptive when it is "elicited under inappropriate stimulus conditons," although the same behavior may be adaptive under different conditions.[10] The following instances illustrate several categories of maladaptive behavior considered in the light of stimulus conditions:

---

[8] Charles B. Ferster, "Positive Reinforcement and Behavioral Deficits of Autistic Children," *Child Development,* Vol. 32, No. 3 (September, 1961), pp. 437-456.

[9] Ogdan R. Lindsley, "Characteristics of the Behavior of Chronic Psychotics as Revealed by Free-operant Conditioning Methods," in Theodore R. Sarbin, ed., *Studies in Behavior Pathology* (New York: Holt, Rinehart and Winston, 1961), pp. 74-87.

[10] Arthur W. Staats and Carolyn K. Staats, *Complex Human Behavior: A Systematic Extension of Learning Principles* (New York: Holt, Rinehart and Winston, 1964), p. 477.

1. Problems of Inappropriate Stimulus Control—situations in which the behavior occurs in response to the wrong stimuli. Psychosomatic illness, in which profound psychophysiological stress may result from social stimuli, and anxiety reactions, in which responses appropriate to noxious stimuli are elicited in response to neutral stimuli, are two examples.

2. Problems of Lack of Stimulus Control—situations in which responses normally under the control of some stimulus fail to occur. The failure of an enuretic child to awaken in response to the autonomic stimulus of bladder distension is an illustration of this category.

3. Defective Stimulus Control—occurs when stimuli control certain categories of response some of the time, but not the entire response class all of the time. For example, antisocial behavior, such as stealing, may sometimes occur despite the existence of verbal proscriptions.

4. Inadequacies in the Individual's Reinforcing System—occur when learning experiences have not provided the opportunities for development of reinforcing stimuli appropriate for behavioral control. For example, Ferster has attributed large segments of the maladaptive behavior of autistic children to their failure to be taught the salience of social mediation. Invalidism as a response to physical illness may similarly be a consequence of the patient's failure to respond to reinforcers that, for most persons, control behavior.

5. Presence of Inappropriate Reinforcers—occurs through "improper learning." In these situations, commonly corollaries of each of the above categories, the individual learns to derive gain from maladaptive responses. For example, the anxiety of the psychotic may be reduced through conversations with imaginary, supportive voices.

BEHAVIOR ASSESSMENT

Assessment in behavior therapy serves the same function as diagnosis in psychotherapy—the collection of data adequate for the formulation of a treatment plan. Behavior assessment differs from diagnosis in at least two respects. First, behavior assessment relies primarily on the identification of observable behaviors, observable reinforcements, and testable inferences about response strength and response flexibility. There are no inferences as to covert psychological structures, motivational concepts in the dynamic sense, or other mentalistic formulations. Second, behavior assessment is directed exclusively toward the collection of data relevant to the solution of problems that are discussed in the treatment contract with the client. The social history common to traditional social casework practice is eschewed because it both leads to the collection of vast quantities of irrelevant data, and it delays the onset of specific problem-solving activities.

Behavior assessment seeks to collect data in two general areas. First, it seeks to identify the precise nature of problem-relevant behavioral *responses* (R). Criteria for determining the limits of such behavior are somewhat ill-defined as yet, but the behavior in question must be related to what is involved in the attainment of the client's goals. Second, behavior assessment seeks to identify the *stimulus* conditions under which the responses currently occur and can be expected to be modifiable. In order to describe the conditions under which problematic respondent behavior occurs, it is necessary to identify the eliciting stimuli (S^E). In order to describe the conditions under which problematic operant behavior occurs, it is necessary to identify the discriminative stimuli (S^D) and the reinforcing stimuli ($S^{R\pm}$). In summary, the data collected must be sufficient to complete the following symbolic statement:

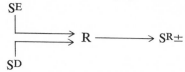

As can be observed, most traditional diagnostic categories are not relevant to behavior assessment. Where categorization occurs, responses are identified as adaptive, maladaptive or missing, while stimuli are identified in the light of their sufficiency for controlling adaptive behavior. Each client is evaluated in light of the ideographic properties of his behavior, beginning with the identification of maladaptive or problem behaviors relevant to specific goals, as determined by the client and significant others in his environment, and then moving toward identification of the steps essential to the attainment of these goals.

PROCESSES OF
BEHAVIORAL CHANGE AND MAINTENANCE

All behavior, adaptive and maladaptive, occurs through the operation of at least two fundamental processes: respondent and operant conditioning. These processes "usually occur simultaneously but involve different responses."[11] *Respondent conditioning* is concerned with the formation of new stimuli for eliciting reflexes already in the individual's repertoire. The reflexes are part of, and are mediated by, the autonomic nervous system through the smooth

---

[11] Thom Verhave, "Introduction," in Thom Verhave, ed., *The Experimental Analysis of Behavior* (New York: Appleton-Century-Crofts, 1966), p. 17.

muscles and glands. In respondent conditioning, the individual learns to respond reflexively to stimuli that did not previously have the capacity to elicit the reflex. The classical example of respondent conditioning is the experiment by Pavlov who trained a dog to salivate (reflex) when a tone (conditioned stimulus) was sounded, after the tone was paired with a taste of food powder (unconditioned stimulus). Both the tone (CS) and the food powder (UCS) are *eliciting stimuli*. Eliciting stimuli are necessary and sufficient conditions for respondent behavior, functioning as triggers for autonomic responses. In most instances a single stimulus yields a single response of comparable intensity, with the impact of the response being seen as changes in internal physiology that are generally behaviorally observable.

The respondent behavior most commonly brought to the attention of the social worker is anxiety. Anxiety occurs in a situation in which an initially neutral stimulus comes to elicit the reaction commonly associated with a noxious stimulus.[12] For example, one who has experienced pain in the dentist's office may experience anxiety when exposed to the eliciting stimulus configuration (dental appartus) that was contiguous with the experience of pain. Anxiety is difficult to overcome because it commonly leads to avoidance responses. In order to avoid the experience of anxiety, the man who fears dentists may not enter a dental office. As long as his avoidance behaviors persist, he is denied the opportunity to learn that his fear may be unfounded. His avoidance behavior is maintained by the fact that it results in the removal of an aversive stimulus—the experience of anxiety. To complicate matters further, it is characteristic of anxiety responses that they readily generalize to stimuli similar to those associated with the origin of the anxiety.

One way to overcome anxiety responses is through the process of counter-conditioning. This is a process designed to neutralize the conditioned association between stimuli when the continued association interferes with adaptation. Wolpe has stated the principle underlying this treatment as follows:

> If a response antagonistic to anxiety can be made to occur in the presence of anxiety-evoking stimuli, so that it is accompanied by a complete or partial suppression of the anxiety responses, the bond between these stimuli and the anxiety will be weakened.[13]

Systematic desensitization is a form of respondent conditioning derived from this principle. In systematic desensitization, the client is trained to relax deeply. He is then presented with feared stimuli in increasing intensities, beginning with very mild presentations. He cannot be both relaxed and anxious at the same time, and relaxation predominates because the aversive stimuli are pre-

---

[12] William N. Schoenfeld, "An Experimental Approach to Anxiety, Escape and Avoidance Behavior," in Paul H. Hoch and Joseph Zubin, eds., *Anxiety* (New York: Hafner Publishing Company, 1964), pp. 70-99.

[13] Joseph Wolpe, *Psychotherapy by Reciprocal Inhibition* (Stanford: Stanford University Press, 1958), p. 71.

sented at low intensities and, for each presentation, the incompatible relaxation responses are stronger. The associations between neutral stimuli and anxiety reactions can be overcome in this manner as new relaxation responses are conditioned to the formerly aversive stimuli. Furthermore, it has been shown that these changes are generally carried over into normal life situations.

As employed in treatment, respondent conditioning takes many forms. It may be used to reduce anxiety, as in treatment to overcome phobias, or it may be used to induce anxiety, as a means of inhibiting antisocial or self-destructive behaviors, such as homosexuality or obsessional rumination.[14]

In *operant conditioning,* the individual emits some behavior already in his repertoire in order to obtain a reinforcement. Unlike respondent conditioning, in which internal changes occur in response to antecedent stimuli, in operant conditioning, behavior designed to change the environment occurs in response to consequent or *reinforcing stimuli.* For example, the young child may be trained to ask for a cookie (a response) in order to receive one (a positively reinforcing stimulus). For this operant conditioning to occur, the behavior of "asking" must exist in his repertoire, it must be emitted, and it must be followed by reinforcement. The reinforcement thus increases the probability of the response. The child might have demanded the cookie rather than asking. This response might have encountered the negative reinforcement of a scolding. To forestall such negative reinforcements in the future, the child might refrain from engaging in any conversations about cookies in the future (response suppression), or he might rely instead upon the prepotent behavior of asking. Through the differential application of positive and negative reinforcements, chains of complex behavior can be developed.

The complexity of behavioral chains can be increased when there is training in the discrimination of situations in which the response is likely to be reinforced. For example, the child might be trained to ask for a cookie when his mother is in the kitchen and not to ask when she is in the tub. Mother's presence in the kitchen sets the occasion for reinforcement, while her being in the tub sets the occasion for the nonoccurrence of reinforcement. Both situations are *discriminative stimuli,* the first setting the occasion for a response that may be met with reinforcement (S^D) and the second setting the occasion for a response that will not be reinforced (S^Δ).

Operant therapy,[15] based on the Skinnerean tradition, consists of the planful arrangement of environments so as to emit specific desirable behaviors. If operant behavior is maintained by its consequences, then alteration of these

---

[14] The reader is urged to consult a review of behavior therapy such as the following: John M. Grossberg, "Behavior Therapy: A Review," *Psychological Bulletin,* Vol. 62, No. 2 (August, 1964), pp. 73-88.

[15] For a comprehensive review of operant conditioning, see: Werner K. Honig, *Operant Behavior: Areas of Research and Application* (New York: Appleton-Century-Crofts, 1966).

consequences must lead to alterations of behavior. The relevant environments might be as narrowly defined as the therapeutic situation or as broadly defined as the total institution. While some transfer of new behaviors is likely to occur, this can be facilitated through the planned extension of treatment through the programming of significant others. For example, if a child is to be taught to control his temper tantrums, his mother and perhaps his teacher must be trained in withholding positive reinforcement, in the form of solicitous attention, when tantrums occur.

Operant therapy can be used to extinguish maladaptive behavior, by allowing it to occur without reinforcement. For example, to achieve extinction the child's mother might ignore his tantrums. Operant therapy can also be used to develop new adaptive behaviors through rewarding selective approximations of a behavioral goal. To achieve this "shaping" goal, the child's mother must positively reinforce each step that the child takes in the desired direction, being careful not to reinforce earlier steps or competing responses. There are many more paradigms of operant therapy, each of which is most generally likely to be effective when the influencee is aware of the objectives and when models of the desired behavior are available.[16]

Operant and respondent conditioning have each given rise to different therapeutic approaches because:

> "So far it has not been demonstrated that operant behavior controlled by its past consequences can be conditioned by means of Pavlov's formula, nor that responded behavior can be manipulated by differential reinforcement contingencies."[17]

This suggests that the operant and respondent dimensions of each case must be analyzed separately. It does not, however, preclude the combination of the two approaches in a single case; indeed, many cases require such handling.[18]

THERAPEUTIC APPROACHES

Given the role of the stimulus determinants of behavior, behavior change can be understood as a process of altering responses to existing stimuli, altering the stimulus field, or altering both responses and stimuli. These three broad approaches can be characterized as follows:

1. The client can learn to *alter his responses to existing forces (stimuli)* in the environment. For example, many young adults fear social con-

---

[16] Albert Bandura and Richard H. Walters, *Social Learning and Personality Development* (New York: Holt, Rinehart and Winston, 1963).

[17] Verhave, *op. cit.*, p. 17.

[18] Arnold Lazarus et al., "Classical and Operant Factors in the Treatment of School Phobia," *Journal of Abnormal Psychology,* Vol. 70, No. 3 (June, 1965), pp. 225-229.

tact with strangers; the sight of a group of unfamiliar persons is thus the stimulus for withdrawal. By learning to overcome this fear, this same group can become the stimulus for approach behavior for the purpose of making new friends.

2. The client can learn to *alter his environment* (stimulus field) so that existing behaviors can yield desired outcomes. For example, the handicapped worker, who unsuccessfully strives for mastery in an occupation for which he is not equipped, can change his area of endeavor. Through this change, the same behaviors that were maladaptive in one setting can achieve success in another setting.

3. The client can learn to *alter both his responses and his environment.* In the complex situations handled by social workers, it is often essential to combine these approaches, in dealing with varied facets of the patient's problem. For example, the mother of a disturbed child might be trained to alter her response to his temper tantrums and might be encouraged to find outside activities to gratify her adult social needs. In other instances, the two approaches might be serially combined in handling a single problem situation, as with the psychotic patient being trained in how to respond to prospective employers and then being exposed to job-finding situations.

CASE ILLUSTRATION

Identifying data: Miss AZ was an unmarried twenty-five-year-old secretary who was referred to Family Service for treatment by the Psychiatric Hospital.

Presenting Problem(s): Miss AZ was referred following hospitalization for a second suicidal attempt. After repair of severely cut arteries, she was discharged from the hospital with a diagnosis of "severe depression." As she viewed her problems, she had cut her wrists because she was very unhappy. Each time that she cut them, she was alone and had been alone for several days, was feeling very depressed and had no plans in the foreseeable future for any activity that might relieve her depression. Being alone and having no plans can be considered to be the eliciting stimuli for the response of depression.[19] Depression, in turn, can be considered to be the discriminative stimulus

---

[19] Depression is understood here to be an autonomic process and as such it is an illustration of respondent behavior. It is also recognized, however, that depression has operant properties such that certain negative affective expressions are emitted and certain classes of adaptive behaviors are not emitted. In both dimensions, the responses are under improper stimulus control and ameliorative responses, are not reinforced by the environment. (See: Charles B. Ferster, "Animal Behavior and Mental Illness," *Psychological Record,* Vol 16, No. 1 [January, 1966], pp. 345-356.)

for the operant behavior of attempting suicide. The expected reinforcement for cutting her wrists was attention from the friend whom she called to help her and from the hospital attendants who treated her; such attention would remove the aversive stimulus of loneliness and also reinforce the suicidal acts.

The problem presented by Miss AZ can be diagrammed as follows:

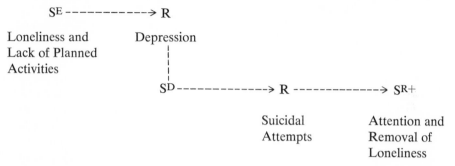

Treatment Goals: The referring hospital sought the prevention of future suicidal attempts. Miss AZ stated that her suicidal attempts were the result of dissatisfaction with her "work, social life . . . everything." She wished to reach a point at which she would be free of depressive and suicidal ruminations, or at least be able to conquer them when they arose. She wished that she could be content with her job, could have friends other than the two middle-aged couples who were her only social contacts, and could be hopeful about her future.

Miss AZ's three problems, while assuredly interrelated, received somewhat differing treatments. Each problem will, therefore, be discussed separately.

Depression and Suicide: (1) Tentative projection of behavioral and environmental changes: Miss AZ first had to become able to control her ruminations when they occurred, and then had to learn to achieve satisfactions in her life sufficient to obviate depression. (2) Relevant conditions and treatment plan: Miss AZ expressed keen interest in religion, reading, and knitting. As she described these prepotent behaviors, religion and reading were clearly dominant. Accordingly, she was given two tasks to perform when she anticipated depression while alone at home; these were to think about the glories of God and how she could help God's will to be done on earth, and to translate selected sections of the *Bible* and the *Apocrypha* into modern English. (3) Rationale: Miss AZ was trained to emit two kinds of operant behavior that would compete with depression. As she could not both glory in the works of God and be depressed, or concentrate upon the meaning of biblical passages and dwell upon her own loneliness, the treatment was systematically geared to forestall depression. Reinforcement for the new responses stemmed from relief of the aversive experience of loneliness, positive reinforcement by the therapist for depression-free periods and energy to engage in other problem-solving activities.

Dull Work Situation: (1) Tentative projection of behavioral and environmental changes: Miss AZ had either to find new satisfactions in her current job or find new work. (2) Relevant conditions and treatment plan: Miss AZ was a trained stenographer but was employed as a posting bookkeeper. She found the work uninteresting and was frustrated by its lack of stimulation. Her goal was to find new secretarial employment involving creativity and social responsibility. She was hindered in attaining her goal because she "feared change" and because she feared that several job changes in the past would label her as a "poor employment risk." Her statement about fearing change was explored objectively (rather than receiving an "understanding" response from the therapist), and she was able to give up such statements immediately. She was then told that the local job market was such that persons of her skill were much in demand and that her work history would not deter employers. The criteria of jobs that would be interesting to her were reviewed and she was aided in determining what she would ask for. Finally she was asked to contact an employment agency within five days and to have at least two interviews within the next ten days. (3) Rationale: Miss AZ fortunately possessed skills much in demand. Had she not been skilled, treatment might have begun with aiding her to locate and undertake appropriate training. It was necessary to help her to overcome her inactivity that was maintained by negative expectations for herself (fear of change) and for prospective employers (who would reject her because of her work history). She was encouraged to assert herself, a counter-conditioning procedure, and was reinforced in this effort with training in specific relevant behaviors (asking for exactly the kind of work that she wanted) and with relevant information about job availability. A schedule was set for her, to enable her to overcome her tendency for inaction. Reinforcement for abiding by the timetable was furnished by the therapist in the form of abundant encouragement and praise, by her own sense that she was taking charge of her problems, and by the promise of new rewards inherent in a new job.

Social Isolation: (1) Tentative projection of behavioral and environmental changes: Miss AZ complained of having no friends her own age and was so fearful of peer contacts that she constantly withdrew from young adults despite her intense desire to be with them. The steps to be taken to accomplish his goal were first becoming as attractive as possible, then locating peers, developing approach behaviors, and developing behaviors appropriate to the maintenance of new friendships. (2) Relevant conditions and treatment plan: Miss AZ expressed herself well and was appropriately responsive to the therapist. She was somewhat unkempt, and specific suggestions were made to improve her appearance. Short-term suggestions included changing her hair style and making her clothing more youthful and attractive. Long-term suggestions centered upon engaging her in a weight-reduction program.[20] It was determined that she possessed basic social skills in ample supply, but that she lacked assertiveness necessary to put her in contact with peers. She was therefore given assertive training which consisted of having her approach one stranger in church and begin a two-sentence conversation, note exactly what aspect of the encounter was anxiety-arousing, and undergo counter-conditioning to overcome this barrier. She was interested in religion, reading, knitting, and swimming and could use these interests to join groups in which she might encounter peers. Furthermore, she expressed an interest in attending college and was encouraged in this direction. As friendships arose, she was guided in means of developing them. During this experience, it was brought to light that since high school, she had never maintained a close contact with a young person within ten years of her age. (3) Rationale: Miss AZ was encouraged to alter her appearance which was an important stimulus for the responses of others to her. For changes made in her appearance, she was reinforced first by the therapist, but more importantly by co-workers and, eventually, by friends. She was given counter-conditioning (assertive) treatment to overcome a respondent condition (anxiety) and then became able to emit a wide range of operant (social approach) behaviors.

DISCUSSION

The main method throughout the treatment process was the issuing of verbal instructions which served as discriminative stimuli ("mands" in Skinner's terms[21]) that set the occasions for the desired behaviors. Suggestions for new behaviors were carefully restricted to occasions in which success was most probable. Success in the mastery of new situations was one important reinforcer for such activities. A second important reinforcer was considerable therapist encouragement prior to each step and praise following each success. A third type of reinforcement was "natural" in the sense that as Miss AZ succeeded in new areas, she created new opportunities for rewards inherent in these areas. A fourth type of reinforcement was the use of concrete rewards. When Miss AZ entered upon a weight reduction program, she was expected to lose an average of one-and-one-half pounds per week for twelve weeks. Each week in which she was successful in losing the predetermined amount of weight, the fee was reduced one-third. She was to put this money in a special place and was to use it to purchase a new dress at the end of the three month

---

[20] Richard B. Stuart, "Behavioral Control of Overeating," unpublished manuscript, 1967.

[21] Burrhus F. Skinner, *Verbal Behavior* (New York: Appleton-Century-Crofts, 1957).

period. These four types of reinforcement explain her "motivation" to participate in treatment aimed at solutions to her own problems.

Treatment for Miss AZ was designed to enable her to overcome numerous behavioral problems. Both operant and respondent procedures were used. Operant procedures are illustrated by training in the use of thinking about God and reading and writing as thought-stopping devices to relieve the stress of morbid ruminations. Other operant procedures ranged from therapist approval for her attempts to change her appearance to the recognition by others of her new, socially appropriate behaviors and the success that she encountered in finding a new job. Respondent procedures are illustrated by training that she received in assertiveness in peer situations that replaced previous anxiety and withdrawal.[22]

One aspect of the verbal interchange deserves special mention. At no time, in the presence of the therapist, was Miss AZ allowed to ruminate about her sad lot. Each time that ruminations began, she was asked to critically evaluate them. Not accepted, they were the subject of critical scrutiny, and their frequency rapidly diminished. In general, such behavior can be understood as operant behavior designed to yield attention.[23]

Treatment might have attempted to relieve her suicidal problem through discussion of the dynamics of her distress. This approach might have achieved success but had two distinct disadvantages. First, she would have been reinforced for continued self-preoccupation. Second, she would have been delayed in taking steps directly relevant to obtaining her objectives. Instead, treatment dealt exclusively with finding a means by which to achieve her goals, thereby helping her to overcome depression through the positive exercise of her capacity for choice.

Miss AZ changed rapidly. Within one week she had already found a new job that provided both more money and a satisfying variety of responsibilities. She began making an effort to extend her social contacts by joining church groups and eventually social groups. She then enrolled in college where she took evening courses for both educational and social returns. She gained no "insight" into inner conflicts through the treatment process, although two other cognitive changes did occur. First, she acquired new labels for her maladaptive behavior. For example, depressed behaviors were "choices" rather than "inevitabilities." Second, she learned to anticipate success rather than failure; that is, there was a shift in her verbalized expectations. It is probable that for two reasons the changes that she has made will be durable over time. First, she has learned reliable new procedures for self-management, procedures whose effect has been made clear to her through experience. Second, she has radically shifted

---

[22] Wolpe, *op. cit.*

[23] Richard B. Stuart, "Casework Treatment of Depression Viewed as an Interpersonal Disturbance," *Social Work,* in press.

her environment. Part of this shift is seen in alterations in her own behavior, an important element in her situation. Part, too, is found in the new people with whom she is in contact, and new circumstances at work and at school in which she finds herself. These new situations provide reinforcement for a new set of behaviors, and it was precisely these reinforcements that were lacking before she undertook therapy.

CONCLUSION

This paper has presented an overview of behavior therapy as it relates to the practice of social casework. The approach is goal-directed and behaviorally specific. It is designed to maintain or change behavior through processes that are identical with the manner in which behavior is acquired. The range of techniques that is available is as broad as the range of problem descriptions. Each technique emphasizes alteration of the controlling conditions of behavior and each, therefore, depends upon precise specification of the problematic behavior, with its antecedent and consequent conditions.

While only one case illustration has been provided, the areas of possible application of the approach are legion. One logical early application can be found in the treatment of "unmotivated" clients who may be socially disadvantaged, severely maladaptive, or strongly disinterested in behavior change. With this group the techniques of behavior therapy provide a technology for promoting engagement in the treatment process. Further extensions might be made to public assistance programs (where recipients might be rewarded for finding jobs rather than punished by reductions in allowances); to correctional settings (where inmates might be rewarded for selective approximations of desired socially adaptive behavior); or to child guidance agencies (where parents might be trained through programming and modeling procedures in more effective child management, and where children might be offered training in the development of missing adaptive skills). There is virtually no area of social behavior not amenable to modification through the application of learning principles, and no setting where this approach cannot be used.

Discussion

Question 1. I am very much impressed with what has been presented and I have been interested in it for a long time. The only thing that I am concerned about is a lack of longitudinal studies. For example, I am aware that the Lovibond procedure for the treatment of enuresis has been used in many cases in New England. Years later, a number of psychiatrists and social workers and child guidance clinics around that region inferred to me that these kids were taking it out in another way. They were just fixing their parents by flunking out of school. Now the reason why I raise this question is that I feel that we have to be sure that the problem that we treat is the central problem in each case. Are you planning any kind of longitudinal studies to evaluate this?

Stuart. This is a reformulation of the symptom substitution argument, and it is well phrased. As Dr. Thomas has indicated, there is little empirical justification for the expectation that symptoms will substitute. There is also rather slight clinical likelihood that this will occur when adequate care is taken in the planning of each case. The problems that are selected for initial treatment are those that have the greatest strategic importance, and/or those that have the most nuisance value. When these problems are successfully managed, some positive transfer to other areas of functioning can be expected. Indeed, there is some clinical evidence to suggest that there is a high transfer of therapeutic effect. There are areas, however, that are not logically related to those selected as an initial treatment focus. It can be expected that problem behaviors in these areas may become manifest, or more correctly may be noticed, when the crisis or nuisance behaviors have diminished. These behaviors can then be treated as they arise. Logically they can thus be better understood as aspects of the initial problem picture rather than as substitutes for successfully treated behaviors.

Now to turn to your question about longitudinal studies. As intense interest in behavioral approaches has been the product of the past decade, the longitudinal literature is relatively sparse. It would indeed be desirable to have long-term studies on the subsequent growth and behavior of children treated with the Lovibond procedure, as an example. But such research must take into account other aspects of the initial problem situation that may have an effect at later stages of development, as well as many situational changes that may occur to the child's deficit during the post-therapeutic period. As the Menninger Foundation research project was to learn, the situational alterations make long-term follow-up studies of psychotherapeutic effects a very complicated research undertaking. Certainly the behavioral group must formulate an intelligent attack upon this problem.

Question 2. I would like to know whether you have had any experience with conjoint treatment using this approach. Have you worked on the problem of several members of a family group? Experience in this area can be of great interest to the profession.

Stuart. Conjoint treatment approaches are implicit in the writings of many behavior therapists including Goldiamond, Lazarus, Wolpe and Ferster. I have had an ongoing opportunity to treat family agency cases over the past several years. In all such cases, the behavior of each family member must be understood in light of the antecedent and consequent behaviors of others. For example, husbands and wives frequently come into treatment saying that the solution to marital discord rests with some change in the behavior of the other. For example, the husband might say, "Everything would be perfectly all right if my wife would go to bed with me," while the wife responds, "I would be very happy to go to bed with him if only he would talk to me more and show greater interest in our home." The solution to problems such as these rests with operant theory which suggests that in order to alter the behavior of another, one must alter one's own behavior. To apply this to the problem marriage, clearly if the husband is to realize his objectives with his wife, he must make social overtures first. If the wife is to increase the frequency of social conversations, she must reduce first whatever behavior on her part that interferes with these conversations. The use of operant conditioning procedures in the treatment of marital and family problems is extremely potent, when each family member is trained to serve as a behavioral engineer for the activities of other family members.

Question 3. My question, I think, is more a basic one. It is, what makes this social work? I say this having come out of graduate work in psychology where indeed I had clinical experience and indeed I learned socio-behavioral therapy. What makes this particularly appropriate as teaching content in a school of social work? Would teaching this content not mean dropping social work as a profession and having all of us move into clinical psychology?

Stuart. It seems to me that socio-behavioral theory provides social work with a technology for the treatment of problems of social adaptation with which the profession has been concerned since its inception. When psychoanalytic theory was adopted as a basis for certain aspects of social work factors, schools of social work did not merge with psychoanalytic training institutes. Just as psychoanalytic theory did not threaten the integrity of our profession, I feel that behavioral theory should not do so. I say this primarily because I am aware of no incongruity between the objectives of behavioral modification as a technology and the value basis of social work.

35

Question 4. It seems to me that what has been considered here are specific ideas about individual and group treatment based on behavioral theory. There are certain questions raised that are not dealt with. How does one go about applying this theory with the client, identifying what the problem is and what the goals are and how they can be achieved? This is at least as important as the treatment techniques that the speakers have elaborated. Second, in Dr. Stuart's paper there was an assumption, not as Dr. Thomas pointed out that behavior is behavior, but that the patient cut her wrists not to commit suicide but because she wanted attention. Does this mean that we are getting into the realm of looking beneath the purpose of behavior? Finally, I think that the example that Dr. Stuart gave of a husband and wife who had difficulty sexually is not a typical case, in that the common basis for goal determination was readily apparent. In many cases, problems are not so apparent. I think that we would need techniques to determine what this common ground is.

Stuart. You've asked three questions, and made several statements. Let me try to respond to your questions in order. First you asked, "How does one determine goals?" Goal determination is a natural process in each case. Goals are inherent in the reasons for the origination of the clinical contact. Somebody sends somebody else for treatment because some aspect of the other person's social adjustment is deemed dysfunctional. Somebody chooses to invest himself in treatment for the same reason, that is, some goal is not being achieved or some problem behavior reoccurs to the individual's disadvantage. Unless goals can be made specific, and unless the goals so identified are congruent with the client's interest, it is unlikely that an effective therapeutic contact can be established.

The second question that you asked dealt with inferences drawn about the motives of behavior. There is nothing mystical inherent in this process. In the case of Miss AZ, I merely asked what she hoped to accomplish. I further asked under what conditions the behavior occurred. I was then able to verify the relationship between the client's conception of antecedent and consequent stimuli by reconstructing with her the actual outcome of her behavior. Equipped with this formulation, I was then able to formulate a series of hypotheses about how this behavior could be effectively controlled. Each hypothesis could be tested, and the results of each of these tests could be used to refine subsequent hypotheses. I therefore built up an understanding of the client's behavior through a series of tested inferences.

The third question that you've raised takes issue with the commonality of the marital problem to which I referred. To this I can say only that my experience has been that some kind of sexual problem coupled with some kind of social problem almost invariably appear in the marital cases who come to me for treatment. In fact, it may well be that the cases coming to the therapist are preselected because of the existence of a shared goal while cases going to lawyers are preselected on the basis of the absence of such goals. If you cannot particularize or objectify the clinical goal in each case, then I feel that you cannot treat effectively. It is a therapeutic task of the first order to enable the clients to clearly state their shared objectives.

Thomas. There are at least three questions tied together here. First, you talked about how do you specify problematic behavior. We talked about that— that behavior has to be identifiable and someone (the client, the helper, or someone else) has to define it as problematic. I don't think there is any great mystery or problem to it.

Secondly, you talked about controlling conditions, such as those for the girl who cut her wrists. Cutting the wrists is a problematic behavior and the reinforcement anticipated for doing so is one controlling condition. Controlling conditions can be identified. They are contemporaneous in the here-and-now environment and we have had various examples of the identification of controlling conditions in the various illustrations considered here.

Third, the question involving the behavioral curricula, the setting of goals, was also illustrated in a number of the cases discussed. The main thing is that you take the existing problematic behaviors and convert them into a behavioral sequence of desirable behaviors, ordering them from the initial, through the intermediate, to the terminal. The point was also made that it may be difficult to isolate the new controlling conditions that we would want to manipulate in order to achieve change—new reinforcers and the like. This is indeed a problem. It is an empirical issue, and I believe we will have to have considerably more research and clinical work in order to isolate these conditions that can exist in a very problematic situation but that are not necessarily readily apparent.

Question 5. Professor Stuart, in your scheme, you talked about a sequence going from behavior, to situations, to personality change. You also talked about social contingencies for behavior. Now there seems to be a contradiction here. You are saying that you first change behavior and then situations will change. This raises a problem in my mind, particularly for people in lower income groups where problem situations are often much more predominant. But even in the case that you presented, what would have happened if your client was unable to find another job?

Stuart. In my initial scheme, I did suggest that if behavior can be altered, then the environment in which the patient lives can change and also if behavior can be altered, ideas about behavior will be changed. Now you are asking what the outcome will be if situations cannot be changed as a consequence of client behavioral changes. To this I can only say that not the patient but the situation should be the target of our objectives. If Miss AZ were unable to find a new job, then I must either help her develop new skills, or help her find a situation in which the skills which she possesses are of some avail. By altering the therapeutic situation, to some degree I can enable her to develop social approach behaviors relevant to job finding. But if these efforts fail and if I can suggest no further modifications in her behavior, then we must look for ways of altering her situation. This might mean moving Miss AZ or it might mean attempting to intervene directly with the environment. For example, it is conceivable that I might have had to mount a campaign to encourage the employment of secretaries who made suicidal attempts.

Question 6. I would like to know whether any of the speakers consider the therapist-client relationship to be of importance. Specifically, would Dr. Stuart have had different results with Miss AZ if he disliked her or if she disliked him? Does this have a place in your theory and was it a factor in this particular situation?

Stuart. Behavior therapy, whether in an individual or institutional setting, clearly involves an interpersonal process. All aspects of the context in which treatment is delivered, and this obviously includes the interpersonal situation, significantly influence the outcome of treatment. Bandura and his associates have done considerable research to identify the characteristics of effective behavior modifiers. Many other researchers are also working in this area. If I had disliked Miss AZ, I would certainly have communicated this in some way. Had she detected dislike, this would have reduced the probability of her emitting behaviors which I desired to promote. I took pains to increase the attractiveness not only of the general treatment situation and our shared change objectives, but also of myself as a therapist. Were I unable to be successful in this aspect of our work, I clearly would have been precluded from success in other areas.

III.
A BEHAVIORAL
APPROACH
TO GROUP TREATMENT
OF CHILDREN

Sheldon D. Rose

Τhis paper presents a description of a behavioral approach for the treatment of children in small groups and some of the practical problems involved in carrying out this model. The approach is characterized by the application of behavior modification precedures and the utilization of the small group as a means to achieve change. There is increasing empirical evidence that behavior modification procedures are highly effective in modifying maladaptive behaviors in a wide range of populations,[1] and considerable research points to the influence of group variables on individual behavior.[2]

One might therefore conclude that the combination of the therapeutic potential of the behavior modification procedures and the small group would enhance present treatment practices. There are only a few studies in which this promising combination has been used.[3] These studies, however, involve

---

[1] See especially Leonard Krasner and Leonard P. Ullmann, eds., *Research in Behavior Modification* (New York: Holt, Rinehart and Winston, 1965).

[2] See Albert H. Hastorf, "Reinforcement of Individual Actions in a Group Situation," in Krasner and Ullmann, *ibid.,* pp. 268-284; William F. Oakes, "Reinforcement of Bales' Categories in Group Discussion," *Psychological Reports,* Vol. 11, No. 2 (October, 1962), pp. 427-435; William F. Oakes, Arnold E. Droge and Barbara August, "Reinforcement Effects on Conclusions Reached in Group Discussion," *Psychological Reports,* Vol. 9, No. 1 (August, 1961), pp. 27-34; David Shapiro, "The Reinforcement of Disagreement in a Small Group," *Behavior Research and Therapy,* Vol. 1, No. 3 (December, 1963), pp. 267-272; Herman C. Salzberg, "Manipulation of Verbal Behavior in Group Psychotherapeutic Setting," *Psychological Reports,* Vol. 9, No. 1 (August, 1961), pp. 183-186; Elaine H. Zimmerman and Joseph Zimmerman, "The Alteration of Behavior in a Special Classroom Situation," *Journal of the Experimental Analysis of Behavior,* Vol. 5, No. 1 (January, 1962), pp. 59-60.

treatment in which the group was used merely as a context, not as an active agent of change, and typically only a narrow range of change techniques was employed. The approach described here endeavors to make greater use of the therapeutic promise of the small group and to employ a large battery of techniques of behavior modification.

Briefly, in this approach, certain therapeutically desirable behaviors performed during the meeting are reinforced with concrete rewards on a systematic basis. Home assignments are given; training is given in the group on how to perform them; and assignments are monitored by the worker through self-report of the child and report of the teacher or parent. Group cohesiveness is stimulated to enhance the power of the group and worker as reinforcing agents and to increase the pressure toward conformity with group norms. Through reinforcement procedures, adaptive group norms and roles are promoted.

It is not possible in the time alloted to this paper to present all aspects of the approach. As a result, some topics have been omitted, and others have been touched on only briefly. We stress such topics as behavioral assessment, monitoring of the change process, token economy, and behavioral assignments. Topics such as the use of the indirect means of intervention have been alluded to only briefly in spite of their importance in this approach.[4]

The approach reported here was first planned in advance. Then, in the course of the summer of 1966, one group was treated using these sets of techniques. On the basis of this experience, in the fall of 1966, eight additional groups were organized, most of them under the auspices of the group work staff of the Hartwig Project of the Neighborhood Service Organization of Detroit. N.S.O. is a multi-function agency that serves children with school adaptation problems, delinquent gangs, clients in housing projects, and clients from other disadvantaged sections of the community. Since N.S.O. has no building of its own, it uses rented office space, store fronts, and school rooms. It has made considerable use of the detached worker who interviews clients and holds group treatment sessions in the homes of clients, at their hangouts, and in local cafes, schools and churches. The Hartwig Project, begun in the fall of 1965, operates out of the precinct police station. The detached worker attempts to use behavioral modification procedures as a means of reducing delinquent behaviors of the children referred by the police.

The groups of clients treated with this approach consist of three to seven

---

[3] See, e.g., Gordon L. Paul and Donald T. Shannon, "Treatment of Anxiety through Systematic Desensitization in Therapy Groups," *Journal of Abnormal Psychology,* Vol. 71, No. 2 (April, 1966), pp. 124-135; Arnold A. Lazarus, Gerald C. Davison and David A. Polefka, "Classical and Operant Factors in the Treatment of a School Phobia," *Journal of Abnormal Psychology,* Vol. 70, No. 3 (June, 1965), pp. 225-229.

[4] For a more complete discussion of indirect means of intervention, see Robert D. Vinter, "The Essential Components of Social Group Work Practice," unpublished manuscript, 1959, pp. 16-25.

children, eight to fifteen years old, who are grouped in such a way as to be relatively homogeneous as to sex, age, and socio-economic background; in most cases, however, the groups are heterogeneous in regard to presenting problems. The clients are, for the most part, referrred to the project after having had one or more contacts with the police for such reasons as prolonged absence from home, breaking and entry, and persistent truancy. Initially, the clients are met by the worker in the police station or, shortly after contact with the police, at home or school. They are told about the group and invited to observe a meeting to see whether or not they would like to join it. Contact with the client may continue on an individual basis if he refuses to visit the group or if no group is available at that time.

BASIC COMPONENTS OF TREATMENT

Basic components of this approach, which form the major subtopics for this section of the paper, include behavioral assessment, establishment of goals, monitoring of change, means of intervention, and termination.

Assessment

The goal of assessment is to determine the nature, frequency, and conditions impinging on the maladaptive behaviors. By "maladaptive," we mean behaviors that need to be increased or decreased in frequency or behaviors that are not being performed in the appropriate situations. Some of the specific problems for which children are being treated are often multiple combinations of the following: truancy, arguments with parents and siblings, non-completion of classroom assignments, glue sniffing, occasional petty larceny, car thefts, absence from the home, limited interaction with other children, avoidance of adults, and sexual aberrations.

Members who are referred to the agency are considered for the group on the basis of behaviorally specific presenting problems. Since, in our experience, most problems can be described in terms of their behavioral manifestations, the worker explores with the client and significant others the complaint made in the referral, the basic behavioral manifestations of that complaint, the frequency of the problematic behaviors, the conditions under which such behaviors occur, and the conditions that appear to maintain those behaviors.

Assessment begins in the first treatment contact with the client and continues, with diminishing emphasis, throughout treatment. The initial assessment is altered, as new evidence for modification accumulates. As evidence is collected, the assessment usually becomes more refined in terms of stipulation of the impinging conditions. As satisfaction from the treatment contacts is experienced, clients and significant others tend to reveal other maladaptive behaviors about which they may have hesitated to speak in the initial contacts with the worker. Moreover, in the group, the worker observes interactive problems that may be an indication of maladaptive behaviors outside the group.

The sources of information about assessment of the problem are the client himself (prior to group treatment); observation by the worker in the group meetings; and interviews with parents, teachers, and other persons relevant to the client. We are also concerned with whom it is who judges the given problem as maladaptive: e.g., client, parent, or teacher. We have found differences among the various people defining the problem even when the evidence is similarly perceived. In some situations, the behavior is defined as maladaptive only by the larger middle class communities and its regulating agencies, the social worker, or the public.

As we pointed out, no assessment is complete with a mere description of the problematic behaviors. It is essential to know the conditions preceding and accompanying the maladaptive behaviors as well as the environmental consequences of the behavior, because the treatment plan is based on this information. Thus, if John sniffs glue several times a week we need to know what happens immediately prior to the sniffing of glue. If we discover that he sniffs glue only when his father leaves him alone in the house, or when he argues with his mother, or if it appears that after he sniffs glue, his younger brothers view him as a hero, there is then a basis for making a treatment plan.

Goal Setting

On the basis of the presenting maladaptive behaviors, individual treatment goals are set for each client in the group. Goals are stated in terms of frequencies or other measurements along the same scale on which the initial maladaptive behavior was established. For example, if Jack went to school on the average of once a week prior to treatment, the ultimate treatment goal might be that he not miss more than one day a month for reasons other than sickness. If the mother has stated that prior to treatment Ted argued with his siblings very frequently, the treatment goal might be that Ted argue with his siblings very infrequently. If Harv can remain sitting in his seat in school only fifteen minutes per hour when it is required, the treatment goal might be to increase that time to 55 minutes.

If the step between the initial performance and the desired performance is not readily attainable, subgoals are established intermediate to the initial level and the final treatment goal. In this way, a series of readily attainable steps are established which are ordered by the client with the help of the worker according to their difficulty of attainment. This sequence is referred to

42

as a behavioral curriclum,[5] one or more of which is established for each client in the group. In the example mentioned above, the worker might set as subgoals for Harv sitting still in his seat 25 minutes in each hour, then 35 minutes and then 45 minutes. The entire sequence, including the terminal goal of 55 minutes, is an example of a behavioral curriculum.

Group treatment goals are established for those interactive problems which most of the members are having. In one group, few of the group members were able to share objects with others. In the first meeting there was not one attempt to share games, food, or other objects with another member. The group treatment goal was to increase the frequency of sharing behaviors to three or more times per meeting. Even group treatment goals, it should be noted, are stated in terms of behaviors that need to be modified.

Tentative, but nevertheless specific, treatment goals are established in the first contacts with all clients. The client is involved in the decision as to which goals and behaviors are to be dealt with. It is imperative in this method that a "treatment contract"—a working agreement as to goals and conditions of treatment—be explored, negotiated, and eventually established with each of the group members. In setting goals, it is necessary to remember that the group must be established both as a source of pleasure and of pressure for change.

Monitoring Behavior

In order to estimate the "intensity" of each presenting problem, it is first necessary to establish a baseline for each of the clients; this baseline is the frequency with which the given problem-behavior is manifested prior to intervention by the worker. The estimate of the baseline makes it possible to evaluate the effects of treatment at any time during treatment.

In our initial group experiences we had planned to establish baseline behaviors from observations made in the group. Since most maladaptive behaviors disappeared after the first five minutes and did not reappear in the five weeks in which the group met, this did not present the best source of observation. Therefore, the baseline is being established in subsequent groups on the basis of parental or teacher reports, or direct observation in crucial situations at home and school. The process whereby observations are made and systematically recorded is referred to as monitoring. Some of the specific techniques used in monitoring have been the use of the Pupil Behavior Inventory[6] and an observational schedule used by volunteer observers in the classroom. In

---

[5] This concept is treated in more detail by Edwin J. Thomas, "The Socio-behavioral Approach: Illustrations and Analysis," pp. 11-12.

[6] See Robert D. Vinter, Rosemary C. Sarri, Darrel J. Vorwaller and Walter E. Schafer, *Pupil Behavior Inventory, A Manual for Administration and Scoring* (Ann Arbor: Campus Publishers, 1966).

addition to these, the teacher or parents may count the frequency of one or more specific behaviors in a given time period, such as the number of fights, the number of times the client argues with the parent, the number of times the client asserts himself to his older brother, the number of hours he spends doing his homework, or the number of days he attends school.

In addition to establishing a baseline, behaviors are monitored at various times during the treatment, at termination, and six months after termination. Some forms of monitoring occur every week in relation to the specific home or school behavioral assignments given to the clients.

The degree of change is estimated by the difference in behavior observed between the period prior to, or at the beginning of, treatment, when the baseline is established, and at the point of evaluation. Thus we have a variety of sources to estimate whether the client is performing at an adequate level and whether he should be completely terminated, partially terminated, continued in intensive treatment, or referred to other agencies.

In addition, we can estimate the stability of change by means of a follow-up evaluation study, six months following termination. School, family, and police data are used to estimate whether changes are stable. Although up to the present time only one group has been terminated to develop procedures for evaluation of the stability of change, we have conducted a follow-up study with clients who had been treated with other methods. Although some refinement is required (such as advising the clients at termination as to our intentions), we were impressed with the possibilities for estimating the effectiveness of treatment in terms of various scales.

Means of Intervention

The generic category for those procedures used to modify client behavior has been referred to as "means of intervention."[7] In the group situation, it is possible to use techniques to modify the ideosyncratic behavior of one individual with little reference to its implication for others in the group. It is also possible to use the same or other techniques for the modification of group attractiveness, group interactive patterns, group norms or rules, and group leadership and status patterns. The former techniques are referred to as direct means of intevention, the latter as indirect. The ultimate goal in both cases, however, is the modification of the behavior of individuals. Behavioral theories have proposed means of intervention, for both direct and indirect purposes, that are highly specific in terms of actual worker behavior. Moreover, in many cases behavioral methods suggest the conditions under which some of these techniques are most useful as well as the ends to which they can best be applied.

---

[7] See Vinter, *op. cit.,* pp. 7-9.

Reinforcement. In this approach, the major means of intervention are reinforcement procedures. In order to establish the worker's potency as a dispenser of both verbal and token reinforcement in the first few sessions, enormous quantities of food (a primary reinforcer) are dispersed to the clients on arrival. Patterson[8] has found that this procedure results in significant responsiveness to the worker, and our initial experiences support his findings. The worker places candy, soft drinks, potato chips, and the like in front of each member as he arrives. "This is just for coming," the worker says. The members usually respond with surprise and even disbelief at which time the worker merely affirms his initial statement. After the third meeting, the reinforcement of this type becomes intermittent,[9] although some type of food may be served on arrival without any statement by the worker.

This not only reinforces the behavior of attending the group meetings, but also establishes the worker as a stronger reinforcer. By being paired with primary reinforcement, he can much more effectively disperse social reinforcement at a later date. Peters and Jenkins[10] have shown that praise by those persons who have previously distributed primary reinforcement is more likely to function as reinforcement than praise by those who have not.

The Token Economy. Most of our clients who come from lower economic subcultures do not initially respond to verbal or social reinforcement. The fact that lower economic groups respond less positively to verbal reinforcement than do middle class groups has been demonstrated by Terrell, Durkin, and Wiesley.[11] For this reason, the major means of reinforcement, in the initial phases of this approach, are tokens. Tokens are given immediately following conformity to group rules, completion of individual behavioral assignments, and performance of any spontaneous behaviors the frequency of which the worker wishes to increase. The extensive use of tokens is generally referred to as a token economy.

---

[8] See Gerald R. Patterson, "A Learning Theory Approach to the Treatment of the School Phobic Child," in Leonard P. Ullmann and Leonard Krasner, eds., *Case Studies in Behavior Modification* (New York: Holt, Rinehart and Winston, 1965), pp. 279-284.

[9] Throughout this paper the reader will note that reinforcement is first used on a continuous basis (i.e., every time the behavior occurs, it is reinforced) and, later, on an intermittent basis (i.e., reinforcement is given on some occasions in which the desired behavior is present and not on others). Behavior which is continuously reinforced is very rapidly added to the repertoire of an individual. But when reinforcement has been terminated, it is also rapidly extinguished. Intermittent reinforcement has been demonstrated to increase the resistance to extinction. For these reasons, we establish behavior with continuous reinforcement and maintain it with intermittent reinforcement.

[10] Henry N. Peters and Richard L. Jenkins, "Improvement of Chronic Schizophrenic Patients with Guided Problem-Solving Motivated by Hunger," *Psychiatric Quarterly Supplement,* Vol. 28, No. 1 (January, 1954), pp. 84-101.

[11] See Glenn Terrell, Jr., Kathryn Durkin, and Melvin Wiesley, "Social Class and the Nature of the Incentive in Discrimination Learning," *The Journal of Abnormal and Social Psychology,* Vol. 59, No. 2 (September, 1959), pp. 270-272.

In our token economy, tokens can be used as money to purchase desirable objects in a "group store." Immediately following performance of the desired behaviors, tokens are administered according to a preconceived plan. The plan involves an appropriate schedule of reinforcement. In such an economy, all behaviors deemed important by the change agents have different numbers of tokens attached to them. Considering the fact that most of our clients suffer from economic deprivation, the tokens are an especially potent form of reinforcement. The group members are told that they are in a group in which they can earn tokens (e.g., chips, painted blocks, paper money) with which they can make purchases from a "store" of items displayed before them. The objects displayed differ in value and include such items as candy bars, model airplanes, cosmetics, tickets to professional sports events, tickets to a beauty show, tickets for a trip with the worker, and credits for purchases at a local snack bar. In addition, a series of catalogues are now being developed which will list objects that can be purchased at later times. Separate catalogues are being developed for boys and girls of different ages.

By performing certain prescribed behaviors or by refraining from performing specified maladaptive behaviors, each member can earn tokens for himself. Tokens are given to a group member after a given time period in which he has adhered to a given rule, spontaneously manifested a desired behavior, or completed his behavioral assignment. Each member keeps his own tokens during the course of the meeting. At the end, he turns in to the worker those tokens that he does not spend in the "group store," and the worker, in turn, keeps them in an envelope. It is important that great care be taken in the bookkeeping because these tokens are so highly important to the members that even minor errors result in emotional outbursts.

Purchases can be made at the end of every meeting. In those groups in which saving is desirable, many highly priced items are placed in the store. (We have contemplated giving interest.) In those groups where members tend to hoard or where it is advisable that the group receive more immediate and frequent gratification, the requirement has been established that half of the tokens earned in a given meeting must be spent at the end of that meeting.

The group remains on the token economy only in the initial phases of treatment. As certain behaviors are reinforced by persons in the extra-group situations, or as the behaviors become self-reinforcing, token reinforcement in the group is gradually removed. At first one activity has no tokens attached to it. Later several activities have no tokens attached to them. When the worker informs the members that the tokens have been removed from the activities, this statement usually provokes a renewal of the discussion of the reasons they are in the group and the ultimate goal of changed behavior without the aid of tangible reinforcement.

It should be noted that the worker does not move directly from token reinforcement to non-reinforcement. Social reinforcement in the form of praise and other forms of recognition are utilized as a consequence of adaptive behaviors on which clients have been working. At first this is on a continuous reinforcement schedule; later the worker moves to a more intermittent schedule in order to establish resistance to the extinction of newly learned behaviors.

Group activities. The group activities are initially planned by the worker in such a way as to facilitate the attainment of the treatment goals. Activities are a means of providing the stimulus conditions for those behaviors which the worker is attempting to modify; e.g., if the worker is attempting to increase cooperative behaviors among members, he may plan as an activity the building of a fort and during the activity he will reinforce all cooperative efforts. Activities may also provide a source of reinforcement just for coming to the group meetings. Since many of our groups consist of children with an extensive delinquent history, it is necessary to find activities which are more attractive than the delinquent activities in which they usually participate. Among the highly valued activities for boys are driving around in the car (when they do not have this opportunity), horseback riding, eating out, riflery, bicycle trips, carnivals, visits to a TV star, or trips. Initially these activities are provided merely as a means of making the group and the worker as attractive as possible. As the group becomes attractive, the worker puts a token value on these activities or makes them contingent on certain performances over a period of time.

In the initial phases of treatment, many varied activities of 10-15 minutes each are used. This enables the worker to provide the stimulus conditions compatible with a number of goals and, at the same time, increases the frequency of the possibility of reinforcement. It also takes into account the limited attention span of most of the clients. As treatment progresses, longer activity periods are added.

Since all of our clients are having difficulties in adapting to school norms, at least one classroom activity is simulated in the treatment meeting. Though the group members initially complain occasionally about this activity, the tokens soon create a work atmosphere. Incidentally, this activity is usually a heavily rewarded one in the first phase of treatment. As the members perceive the results of improvement in school, the teacher's verbal rewards are usually sufficient to sustain the behavior. The activities used may be such things as, (1) writing an essay about a picture that the worker presents, (2) reading quietly or talking only after the worker-teacher calls upon him, or (3) solving a a simple arithmetic problem. During the simulated schoolroom activities, the worker assumes much of the role of the teacher. He becomes stricter, demands more attention and, in general, tries to recreate the classroom atmosphere.

Delinquents not only lack skills for adapting to the demands of the classroom; most also lack sports or other physical recreational skills. Few sources of satisfaction, other than delinquent activities, are open to them. For this reason, a physical activity is also included in each meeting. The worker usually spends at least a part of the time devoted to this activity training the members in the performance skills. In complex sports activities it may be necessary, initially, to simplify the game and the number of rules in order to avoid excessive frustration. Too many rules for many of our clients provide the stimulus conditions for highly aggressive behaviors. In the course of treatment, however, a conscious effort is made to increase their skills and the rules and complexity of the games.

Initially, the worker selects the activities according to his knowledge of developmental and sociological taste patterns of his group members. There is little choice by the group members, most of whom are deficient in decision-making skills. Of course, there is some feedback, which the worker later uses to modify the program. As the group builds a repertoire of activities, members are allowed to choose their activities as they learn the skills of choosing. The worker may have to include many activities the clients do not prefer as a means of creating conditions for increasing or decreasing certain types of behaviors. The worker makes the ultimate decision as to the nature of the program utilized. Obviously, this is a highly complicated process, and the worker must be careful to balance attractive activities with the less attractive ones, if he does not wish to make the group aversive. It is interesting to note that, in most cases, if there is self-improvement in the skills required to perform the activity, even aversive activities become attractive.

Behavioral Assignments.   A set of behaviors assigned by the worker or members of the group to a given client with his concurrence and participation is a behavioral assignment. These behaviors are expected to be performed in a given time period, usually prior to the next group meeting or conference. These assignments are directly related to the treatment goal and may represent a subgoal or intermediate goal that the client needs to attain prior to the attainment of one of the ultimate treatment goals. Since much of the behavior that social workers are attempting to modify does not occur within the context of the treatment group, this technique is an excellent means of giving the client practice in the desired behaviors or in restraining or controlling himself from participation in undesirable behaviors in a broad range of situations. Some examples of behavorial assignments are the following:

Walter, who skips school on the average of twice a week, is assigned the task of attending school for four complete days in a row. Frank, who has frequent arguments with his parents over the fact that he comes in after ten o'clock every night, is assigned the task of coming in at least two nights before ten o'clock and reporting back to the group and the worker the reactions of the parents. Anita, who seldom asserts herself in situations outside the group, has recently begun to do so in the group. The group members assign her the task of responding to her sister, who con-

48

stantly criticizes her clothing. Anita must say, "It's my clothing and my taste, and I'll wear what I want."

Initially the behavioral assignments are given solely by the worker. As the group members learn the criteria for the establishment of an assignment, they participate not only in their own assignment, but in the assignments of others in the group. The group members also participate in judging whether or not a given assignment has been completed.

Obviously, the effectiveness of such an assignment is dependent on a number of factors. First, the assignment must be highly specific. The client must not only know what he must do; he must know the conditions under which he should do it. Furthermore, if certain unexpected conditions (such as illness) arise, or if the stimulus conditions do not occur, alternative behaviors, such as calling the worker, should be specified. If the assignments are too vague, the client can hedge, the monitoring becomes difficult, and change can scarcely be estimated.

Second, if success is to be obtained, the behaviors should have a relatively high probability of being carried out. If an assignment is given not to argue with mother and she was away on vacation the week following the assignment, failure to perform in the required manner would be certain. If the assignment to the client is, "If someone fights with you, walk away," he will be unable to perform the assignment in the course of the week if no one initiates a fight. Should the shy girl be given as a first assignment standing up to her older brother who bullies her, chances of success are low.

If tokens are administered for successful completion of an assignment, monitoring of the assignment by means of direct observation or the report of significant others is usually desirable. If not, the worker may be put in a position of reinforcing exaggerated accounts or lying. Where monitoring is not possible or where monitors may be unreliable or uncooperative, assignments may be given for which no token reinforcement is used. If only verbal reinforcers are used, our experience seems to suggest that the likelihood of deception in self-reports is highly reduced. Praise, it seems, functions as a reinforcer only when the client feels it is deserved.

As one assignment is completed, a slightly more difficult one should be given. Each assignment should be sufficiently difficult so that the client has to make some effort to accomplish it, but sufficiently within the reach of the client so that success is highly probable. As has been frequently noted, success in change is a potent reinforcement in the change process. But if the assignment involves no change at all, we have reinforced only behaviors which are already in the client's repertoire.

If the client states that he is unable to perform a given assignment because he does not know what he should do, or if he is frightened or shows discomfort or a lack of clarity about the procedures to be followed, the worker can reduce the discomfort in a number of ways. He may utilize group discussion with the other members of the group, especially those who have already performed the behavior under the stipulated conditions. He may demonstrate or ask one of the group members to demonstrate exactly how it is to be performed. The worker may use behavioral rehearsal in which first the worker or a peer demonstrates, and then the given client practices the behavior to be performed. When direct practice is not possible, the worker and peers may describe to the client specific steps he must take. One child who had the assignment of being home by 9 p.m. and remaining there was taunted by the other children standing out on the street until he finally went out again. The worker asked the group how they thought he should handle the situation. After they made some suggestions, one of the children played the role of the given client, and the worker and several of the other children played the roles of the children on the street. Finally, the given client played his own role. This example demonstrates the use by the worker of a combination of techniques to insure successful carrying out of the assignment.

Instead of, or in addition to, the techniques described above, the worker may modify the environment itself, so that the probability of success is increased. In the case of a teacher who criticized the client unmercifully whether or not he changed, the worker arranged for an observer to sit in the class that particular week. The presence of the observer seemed to be a sufficient condition to soften the teacher's constant criticism. In the case of a client who had never been able to do his homework, the worker arranged for a tutor to help him.

A third general requisite of success is to be sure that reinforcement follows immediately after the response one wishes to modify. When assignments are used, the reinforcement for their completion usually occurs at the meetings. There are several ways to deal with this problem. First, the teacher, the mother, or the tutor, gives a note to the child to give to the worker. The note for some children may function as sufficient immediate reinforcement. In some cases the workers have had the significant others who monitored the behavior reinforce the client on the spot with tokens or praise. For assignments in which the given behaviors must increase or decrease over a given time period, the worker stated that the "fixed interval" terminated at exactly the moment that the group meeting began. Where this was not feasible, a special meeting in the middle of the week was arranged in which reinforcement for the completion of short-term assignments was distributed.

Model Presentation. In order to facilitate the learning of new behaviors, real or symbolic models may be presented to clients under those conditions which facilitate social imitation. Since a number of empirically supported hypotheses exist as to the modes and conditions of model presentation that optimize the possibility of imitation, these hypotheses can function as operational guidelines for the worker. Some examples of these hypotheses that will be discussed below include the use of role-playing, the use of rewards for the model in the presence of the imitator, the use of high status persons as models from the subculture of the imitator, and the use of films or other sources of symbolic models.

One planned form of model presentation is role-playing which has been frequently demonstrated to facilitate learning. In one type of role-playing, the model (a peer or the worker) performs the role of the client under conditions that stimulate the conditions in which the client is having difficulty. There are many ways of optimizing learning in role-playing. One of these is to replace the worker with the peer as model as soon as a peer is capable of performing this role. The more the stimulus conditions approximate those of real life, the higher the probability of imitation of the model.[12] This hypothesis points to a second form of optimizing learning. Aspects of the role-playing should duplicate as nearly as possible real life situations. For example, role-playing in the home is more effective than role-playing in a treatment center or school building; the use of the real sibling is preferable to the use of the imitated sibling. A third way to increase the effectiveness of role-playing is to reward the model for performing the appropriate behaviors. Bandura and Walters report that if the model is rewarded in the presence of the subject, the probability of imitation by the subject is increased.[13] Fourth, the individual should move from observing to performing newly learned role behaviors under the simulated conditions, and finally a series of behavioral assignments can be used to encourage the individual to perform the newly practiced behaviors in real life situations such as the home, school, playground, or local hangout.

Another procedure based on the above-mentioned hypotheses that we have used is the introduction into the group of guests who are particularly attractive to the group members. Examples of these models are athletes, a TV disc jockey, and a popular teacher. In order to provide more than a model for general orientation to life, which the worker is also providing, the models are programmed to discuss the "moral dilemmas" with which they were confronted in their adolescence and how they resolved these in a pro-social way. Sports heroes reward the group by giving the members sport lessons. Members have their picture taken with the TV disc jockey. The rewarding by the model of the group increases the probability of the group members imitating the behavior or verbalizing the particular orientation.[14] As the members progress, models are used who have made life choices similar to the ones the

---

[12] For a discussion of this hypothesis, see Arnold P. Goldstein, Kenneth Heller, and Lee B. Sechrest, *Psychotherapy and the Psychology of Behavior Change* (New York: John Wiley and Sons, 1966), pp. 217-219.

[13] Evidence for this hypothesis is discussed in Albert Bandura and Richard Walters, *Social Learning and Personality Development* (New York: Holt, Rinehart and Winston, 1963), pp. 81-82.

[14] *Ibid.*, p. 83.

group members have stated they might like to make. These have been such persons as technicians, cooks, labor organizers, youth leaders, a manager of a roller skating rink, a dental assistant, and a civil rights organizer.

A more spontaneous means of increasing imitation of behaviors that the worker is trying to increase among one or more members of the group is accomplished by the instantaneous rewarding of the desirable behavior performed by a high status group member in the presence of the other group members.

In a group of highly aggressive youngsters, Pete, the informal leader, was one of the two who was seldom provoked to fighting. Nevertheless, when Charlie bumped into him, Pete was rewarded by the worker for walking away. The purpose was not to increase the probability of this behavior in Pete under the same circumstances, but to increase the imitation of these behaviors by others. In the same group Fred, a low status individual, never fights either. Yet he would not be rewarded under the same circumstances.

Another form of model presentation involves the use of films in which the hero performs those behaviors that the worker would like some members to imitate; the worker may point out those behaviors; he may involve the group in the discussion of the behaviors; or the discussion may pave the way for the role-playing sequence discussed above. Discussion is concerned not only with the behaviors worthy of imitation but also with those behaviors that are followed by immediate or long-range aversive consequences.

A major problem of treatment groups either in institutions or in out-patient groups such as ours, is the presence of many anti-social models. Maladaptive behaviors may thus be seen, practiced, and reinforced. Since modeling affects occur whether the treatment personnel intend them or not, it is imperative that the clients be provided with new and, hopefully, exciting models in a more systematic way than the neighborhood, group, or institution can provide. As Bandura points out, "The systematic use of modeling techniques, whether singly or in conjunction with other treatment methods, is likely to accelerate substantially the successful achievement of therapeutic outcomes."[15]

Other Treatment Procedures. In addition to the behavior modification procedures already mentioned, a number of other procedures have been used to treat special problems not amenable to previously discussed techniques. One such procedure is covert sensitization.[16] This has been used in our groups in the treatment of lying behavior and compulsive stealing.

---

[15] See Albert Bandura, "Behavioral Modification through Modeling Procedures," in Krasner and Ullmann, *op. cit.,* p. 340.

[16] For a discussion on one variation of this technique, see Joseph R. Cautela, "Treatment of Compulsive Behavior by Covert Sensitization," *Psychological Record,* Vol. 16, No. 1 (January, 1966), pp. 33-41.

Because of the presence of a number of anxious clients, the staff of the project is being trained in reciprocal inhibition procedures, i.e., procedures whereby responses that are incompatible with anxiety are stimulated in the client.[17] Two techniques used are systematic desensitization, based on relaxation, and "emotive imagery."[18] In the former, the client is confronted with the fear-stimulating object in increasing intensities while playing some exciting game or imagining some exciting event, such as pretending that he is Batman and is seated in a Batmobile. In this case, anxiety is incompatible with the emotions aroused by exciting play. Since Lazarus has demonstrated the effectiveness of the former procedure with groups of clients,[19] we would assume that both procedures could be utilized within the context of the operant group. Although this has yet to be demonstrated in our groups, desensitization procedures have resulted in reduction of anxiety or fear in several cases.

Because we are in the first phase of our project, we have not as yet at our disposal all the procedures that our presenting problems require. Although we are rapidly expanding our use of various combinations of procedures reported here, we are confronted with some problems for which our techniques at their present stage of development are not completely adequate. Continued innovation and experimentation with new behavioral technology is thus required.

Termination

Termination in this approach is considered on the basis of the achievement of treatment goals. Since there is an ongoing monitoring of the change process, it is possible to estimate at what point termination should take place. When termination is being considered, all sources of information are recontacted, and based on the information accumulated, a decision is made as to whether treatment should be continued or the client partially or completely terminated, or referred to other agencies.

One of the problems of termination in most of group treatment derives from the fact that most clients become attached to the group and the worker during treatment. Yet, in order to terminate a client, he must be able to function independently of worker assistance in a school, family, work, or recreational setting. This implies that prior to termination the worker assists the client to find other more useful sources of support in teachers, friends, a local minister, boy's club, or parents; and assignments are usually given to

---

[17] For a detailed account of the reciprocal inhibition hypothesis and treatment procedures derived from this hypothesis, see Joseph Wolpe and Arnold Lazarus, *Behavior Therapy Techniques* (Oxford: Pergamon Press, 1966).

[18] The most extensive account of emotive imagery is to be found in Arnold A. Lazarus and Arnold Abramovitz, "The Use of 'Emotive Imagery' in the Treatment of Children's Phobias," in Ullmann and Krasner, *op. cit.*, pp. 300-304.

[19] *Ibid.*

this end. He is encouraged and, if necessary, trained to make friends who live in his neighborhood or go to his school. The transfer of change to situations outside of the group is also carried out on a planned basis in order to insure success.

CONCLUSIONS

Although the data that have been collected after several months of operation with the behavioral approach to group treatment are necessarily limited, the results thus far seem to be promising. Changes in the desired direction have been observed for the large majority of male clients who have been treated from two to four months. In almost all groups, the behavioral assignments have been positively received by group members and, in most cases, carried out. In no groups has there been unplanned discontinuance. The group workers, all of whom are using this approach for the first time, seem to be enthusiastic about it. Moreover, they seem to be rapidly developing a large body of communicable skills that hold the promise of still greater effectiveness. They are coaching volunteers and other non-social work trained workers in the various techniques. Other agencies in the city area are beginning to explore the use of these procedures.

Of course, there are still problems. With those delinquent adolescent girls who are dependent on highly complex family situations, progress has been slow, especially where the parents have refused to cooperate. At present we still have an insufficient number of terminated cases to estimate the degree of stability of change. We have, as yet, no control data to discover whether the changes we have observed are not due to maturational changes or to various non-specific aspects of treatment. Thus far, we have not always collected our data in our own prescribed systematic manner. Some of our impressions are, no doubt, colored by our enthusiasm for the method. Hopefully, our ongoing research will soon contribute to clarification of at least some of the many questions that are still partially or totally unanswered.

Discussion

Question 1. If in relation to goal formulation, the end goal includes behavioral changes in individuals, then the group is the context and the means of change. If, however, the end goal is group function, would your plan of intervention be changed? For example, suppose your end goal is that the particular group become a reference group for nondelinquent subcultures. Would your plan of intervention change?

Rose. Our approach to treatment has been to focus primarily on individual behavioral change because the treatment group, by necessity, would be broken up after 16-30 weeks, by which time we hope to have attained the individual treatment goals. At termination, we no longer want the treatment group to be maintained as a reference group. One of the behavioral assignments is that, as the group approaches termination, each member explore joining such groups as the Boy Scouts, recreational groups of service organizations, and the Y.M.C.A. What we ultimately try to do is find them new reference groups to supplant the treatment group. Although during treatment the group may serve as a reference group, the end goal is never to establish the treatment group as the final reference group.

Question 2. I would be interested in knowing if, before the group starts making behavioral assignments, the therapist gives an assignment directly to a member, or does he try from the very beginning to get the group to do it.

Rose. We utilize the principle of "successive approximation" that Dr. Thomas mentioned. Since each client ultimately will have to be his own behavioral modifier, he must learn to be able to give himself behavioral assignments. Because most clients initially lack the essential skills, the worker trains them first by means of model presentation or demonstration. Then, as a member learns the criteria, he is asked to develop his own assignment with the assistance of the other members. The worker, however, maintains a veto that, to my knowledge, has seldom been used.

Question 3. Oh yes, one follow-up question on that. Would you comment on how you keep the group involved in the process when you get into a dialogue with the one person to work out a behavioral assignment?

Rose. There are two ways of involving the members. The first is merely to ask the other members if they think the assignment is too easy, too hard, too weakly rewarded, etc. The second procedure is to use tokens to reward comments by others on a given person's assignment. In those rare instances where the first is inadequate, the second is almost always sufficient to get broad participation.

Question 4. Are you satisfied with solving a series of continuing behavioral problems? For example, you say we give assignments but we let the people decide whether they want to carry out these assignments. At the same time, you say that you use the power of the group to pressure members to conform to group norms. What is the area of the client's freedom? Is it the right to concur or not as they wish?

Rose. We too are concerned with the client's freedom—especially his freedom to make choices among several alternatives. How much freedom does he have to refrain when the gang agrees to break into a garage? How much freedom does he have with a passive, nondirective, or non-goal-oriented group worker when the client lacks the skills either to distinguish alternatives or to make choices? In the former situation, he may be "bullied" into action; in the latter, he may be "contaged." In our groups we modify conditions which facilitate his learning how to recognize and choose alternatives. The major influences are reinforcement and group pressure. We teach problem-solving skills step by step. As he acquires them, he gradually increases the activities he performs himself and the decisions he makes about his own present and future. No child can do this at once, yet this, in a sense, is what one expects when the client is overwhelmed with "freedom" without the knowledge of how to use this freedom.

Vinter. No one has directed a question to me, but I have a response to make. I think that perhaps it hasn't been made sufficiently clear that the kinds of problems behaviors being referred to here may be of fundamental import for the individuals involved. This is not simply a matter of "symptom relief" or less discomfort. For example, take the youngster in the public school who continuously engages in the wrong behavior and, consequently, is regularly thrown out of the class and, ultimately, suspended. Through methods such as the ones discussed here, he can be helped to modify those particular behaviors that affect his continuation in school and his chances of benefiting from the education in later life.

Question 5. What is the selection process for the group? Do you take everybody who is referred to you by the police? Do you examine the motivation for change on the part of these delinquents, or do you take them even though they are indifferent and don't want to change their behavior?

Rose. We try to take every child into treatment who is referred by the police. Some children are not put into a group if there is no one in their neighborhood who is approximately the same age or if other conditions of adequate group composition are not met. When we are not able to group the child in a way that we think would be effective, we use individual treatment methods. We have contact with the children just after they get in trouble with the police and we note that their motivation to change is higher in many cases than one might expect from youthful offenders. Some children, however, who seem to identify us with the police, do not enter into treatment. Others, who also view us as police, come initially because they feel they must. Some children are willing to visit a group meeting "just once" to see what it is like; they usually return after they experience the token economy. In general, with "low motivation" clients, the initial contract is merely an agreement for them to explore whether or not we have anything to offer. Later, the contract may be ended or, more usually, renegotiated in an agreement to work on behavioral change.

I should add that in respect to referrals, there is preselection by the police. Thus far in our project, the police have not referred many so-called hard-core delinquents because these children are usually handed over immediately to the courts. Although multiple-offenders are referred to us, they are usually guilty of a series of minor offenses. For this reason, in the large majority of the cases, some discomfort concerning present behavior can be noted. This discomfort provides the essential motivation required for treatment.

Question 6. How does your system apply to groups of clients who do not perceive their behavior as being critical or problematic? For example, suppose we see a bunch of kids in a given community who are eleven years old, and it appears to us they are moving toward delinquent behavior. We could pretty well predict that in two years they are going to get into trouble with the police. They may end up in reform schools. But by the standards of the community in which they live or the nature of the activities in which they engage, their behavior is not specifically problematic. They have no sense that their behavior is problematic. How would you proceed in this case?

Rose. This is a very important question. If there is no sense of problem at all on the part of the child, we probably would have difficulty in treating him on an outpatient basis with this method. However, in our experience, even the hard-core delinquent who is allegedly totally identified with the delinquent norms also has some societally compatible attitudes, values, and behavior. Although in early contacts he may try to cover these, it usually becomes apparent that he would like certain material benefits or forms of approval which can be derived from the normative culture. He may want to avoid some of the obviously aversive consequences—such as fear, physical pain, referral to a training school—of his acts. Some of the clients around thirteen or fourteen years of age, for example, are concerned about getting jobs for which only a technical school diploma will make them eligible. Others have heard from their older brother, cousin or friend about how it was in the Boys' Training School. Although many clients say that they don't want what the social worker is selling, they come to the group anyway to find out what alternatives are open to them. Wherever possible, we use reinforcers to promote exploration with us of their alternatives. We use confrontation with ultimate aversive consequences as another procedure to dramatize alternatives. For example, we may go with clients to the Boys' Training School. By exploring new behaviors and comparing these to present behaviors and their consequences, alternatives become apparent. It is only at the point when they agree there is something they want, that we are able to take the next steps. I think that the desire for change is present to some degree in almost every child with whom we have had contact so far. Some need more time than others before they show it.

Question 7. Are you saying that, in a sense, your technique for this type of population is to impose on them a sense of crisis?

Rose. Yes, in a sense, this is what I am saying. In almost all treatment methods, some anxiety or even a sense of crisis is created in clients, either inadvertently or on a planned basis.

Vinter. In another series of efforts with groups in the schools, none of the hundreds of youngsters at all grade levels, in all classes and of both sexes, that we worked with who were officially identified by the school as approaching or already in trouble, ever denied it. They had awareness and concern about it because they get "clobbered" by authorities.

Thomas. We are coming dangerously close to inferring here, from the Stuart and Rose presentations and from the discussion, that the client must always define his own behavior as problematic in order to make use of the socio-behavioral approach. There are always at least three different sets of definers for problem behavior: the client himself, the worker, and other people. I am sure that we are going to be using the socio-behavioral approach with some persons who do not define their behavior as problematic. Take the case I described of the young child who had tantrums. The child didn't say, "I have a problem and I want to be helped," and the child was not consulted concerning his willingness to stop having tantrums. We will continue to have to work with some persons whose behavior is initially defined as problematic mainly by others, not by themselves. There is no reason of which I am aware to restrict the socio-behavioral approach exclusively to clients who define their own behavior as problematic.

58

IV.
APPLICATIONS OF SOCIO-BEHAVIORAL THEORY
TO ADMINISTRATIVE PRACTICE[1]

Roger M. Lind

This paper is part of a broader discussion of socio-behavioral theory in the practice of social work. Much of the prior discussion was concerned with its use in situations involving interpersonal treatment. In this paper, the utility of socio-behavioral theory for administrative practice will be explored. Case examples will be used to illustrate the applications and to provide accurate basis for a more general discussion.

Administrative practice, especially in its interpersonal aspects, is concerned with facilitating the acquisition of needed skills and habits, the strengthening of such capabilities already possessed, the maintenance of desired performance in the organization, and the weakening or elimination of behaviors seen as dysfunctional to the organization. Supervisors and employees are almost inevitably involved in these matters, either in one-to-one situations or as members of a group.

BEHAVIOR MODIFICATION WITHIN ORGANIZATIONS

In the context of behavior modification within organizations, two important problem areas will be considered: individual malperformance in committees, and employee difficulties handled directly by the supervisor.

Committee Behavior

The first example is taken from a paper by a community organization student[2]

---

[1] Acknowledgement is made of the helpful review and substantial critical comments and suggestions made by Alan Haber and Willard J. Maxey, Jr.

[2] Alan Haber, "Operant Conditioning in a Committee: A Case Example," unpublished manuscript, 1966. The reporter will be referred to as the change agent.

who reports on the use of specific techniques to change the behavior of members of a committee in which he was functioning as participant-observer. The community committee consisted of low-income people attempting to mobilize resources for self help. The change agent became concerned because the committee was not achieving its objectives. Meetings were attended by a core of regulars and a floating body of intermittent attenders. The regulars dominated meetings, and the others rarely spoke.

The change agent identified five "problem behaviors" in meetings:

1. People tended to interrupt each other.
2. They didn't listen when others spoke.
3. The meeting frequently broke down into "cross-talk" and discussion between neighbors.
4. Speakers rambled in the course of their speaking, and freely changed the subject.
5. The chairman was not successful in maintaining control or an ordered flow of discussion.

These behaviors did not contribute to the group's accomplishing the tasks it had before it. But given that the appropriate behaviors were available to the participants or, if not, could easily be established, the job of the change agent was to design a regimen of behavior modification by which the desired behaviors could be substituted for current ones.

The three changes the agent wanted to accomplish were (1) to end cross talk and interruption, (2) to link hand raising and requests for recognition, and (3) to limit length of discussion.

The specific behaviors to be established were as follows:

"1. That people raise their hands to talk;
2. That people not talk until called on by the chairman;
3. That when the person recognized by the chair is talking, other people not talk;
4. That people not talk more than three minutes;
5. That people not raise their hands until the speaker has finished or has talked three minutes."[3]

As the change agent viewed the situation, he possessed two special tools: his tape recorder and note pad. These tools were indeed "special" in the context in which he was operating. He was recognized as the analyzer, historian, and "recorder for posterity," for the sessions of the group. In short, he was a high status person paying attention to what they said and did. The members noticed what the student did when he attended their sessions, and his attention was reinforcing for them. Members would suggest, as they made what

---

[3] *Ibid.*, p. 1.

they considered important points, that he make a note of them ("Write that down"), or they might inquire whether the recorder was on. Thus, taking or not taking notes and recording or not recording, in this context, provided the group members with positive or negative reinforcement.

There were five ways in which these techniques of influence were used:

1. When someone raised his hand, the change agent looked his way, smiled and made a note on his pad (positive reinforcement).
2. When someone who was called on spoke, the change agent looked his way, turned on the recorder, and took notes on what he said (positive reinforcement).
3. When a speaker was interrupted or there was cross-talk, the change agent switched off the recorder (the "click" was easily heard), and made clear that he was not paying attention to what was being said (averted head, changed position, stopped making notes) [punishment].
4. When interruption or cross-talk stopped and the speaker continued or the chair recognized another, the change agent switched on the recorder and resumed taking notes attentively (positive reinforcement).
5. The change agent also served as a model by participating in those ways he was attempting to reinforce: raising his hand, speaking only when called upon, and limiting the length of his remarks (modeling).

Although he did not discuss his efforts with anyone in advance, the change agent did talk with the chairman about using the raised hand as the basis for recognizing a speaker, discouraging cross-talk, and limiting the length of individual speeches; he also helped the chairman to plan meeting agendas and clarify issues and objectives.

Having established which behaviors to weaken and to strengthen, the change agent then had to select which behaviors to change first. He deferred the question of the length of time one talked in order to deal first with interruptions, cross-talk, and connecting the raised hand and the open mouth. Without going through the entire procedure, let us refer to some of the efforts and their consequences.

The author, Haber, indicates that his behavior was an attempt to use punishment and negative reinforcement to weaken the cross-talk, and positive reinforcement to encourage the association between raising the hand and speaking when recognized. His way of giving or withholding attention was important to the speaker, but apparently had little direct effect on the group as a whole. Speakers would respond by criticizing those who interrupted them. Although the direct effect was weak, the indirect effect was the establishment of a norm of non-interruption which was supported by the members. The intervention of the change agent was an appeal to the norm, and this stimulated others to invoke it.

The operation aimed at shaping speaker behavior in the direction of speeches of shorter length has a similar history, and, therefore, will not be repeated here. The author reports that the desired behaviors were well-established in three to four sessions.[4] His evaluation was based on unsystematic observation and, in this respect, does not meet the general requirements of the socio-behavioral method. Close, accurate, and specific observation of the behavioral outcome would have been desirable.

This example is considered important enough to treat at some length because it illustrates the several steps in the application of the socio-behavioral approach. The example also demonstrates how various intrinsic reinforcers, those already available in the situation, may be carefully employed to alter behavior toward desired ends and, in this case, without the persons being aware of this use. Thus a committee chairman or executive may use such a mundane practice as note taking as a mean of reinforcing behavior.

The second example is taken from an unpublished paper by Maxey on a series of three efforts to alter executive behavior.[5] In contrast to the first example, this one focuses on the behavior of one staff member rather than all the members of the group. While the foregoing example illustrates the ingenious exploitation of strong incidental reinforcers, this and the following examples demonstrate that there are at hand such common reinforcers as approval and attention that can be manipulated directly and explicitly, through simple interaction, and without special equipment.

This situation involves a staff member whose behavior the change agent characterized as displaying "insufficient manifestation of verbal behavior in situations requiring exchange of information." Considered bright, energetic, and highly experienced and trained, this person provided valuable information when he did speak up. For this project, the outline of current conditions and proposed intervention was as follows:

Baseline information: Uses 25 percent of equivalent time[6] to talk.
Intermediate objective: Uses 50 percent of equivalent time to talk.
Desired goal: Uses 100 percent of equivalent time to talk.
Change techniques were that the agent should:
    1. Pay strict attention to the subject when he is speaking. Show this
    by making eye contact;

---

[4] Although impressed with the effectiveness of the techniques, the change agent chose to discontinue the intervention because it began to hamper his functioning as research observer, the student's primary function in that group.

[5] Willard J. Maxey, Jr., "A Use of Socio-Behavioral Theory in Administration," unpublished manuscript, 1966.

[6] "Equivalent time" was measured as the number of minutes duration of the meeting divided by the number of participants, excluding the agency director. The measure is based on equal participation by all members.

2. Give motor and verbal cues (such as nodding head in agreement, saying "good point,") to subject when he talks; and

3. Compliment and praise subject for his comments in the discussion following meetings and in one-to-one conferences.

The technique used here is positive reinforcement, with attention, agreement, and approbation serving as the reinforcers. The alteration the change agent desired to make was an increase in the subject's verbal participation in meetings. The employee showed the behavior occasionally, and the change agent made available to him both the reinforcers and the opportunity to use them.

Assessment of experience during the second week of intervention showed the non-talker to have participated 76 percent of his "equivalent participation time." A brief follow-up monitoring undertaken three months after the project's end showed that he was functioning at 60 to 65 percent of "equivalent time." This represented a decline from the level of participation achieved in the second week of intervention[7], but is a level much higher than the baseline of 25 percent.

Supervisor-Employee Relations

Prior examples deal with behavior which is administratively inappropriate or inefficient, and which impedes the realization of agency goals. Thus far only group situations have been considered, but it is equally possible to demonstrate the utilization of socio-behavioral techniques in interpersonal relations of supervisor and employee. The Maxey report[8] describes such a situation and the intervention techniques used in order to produce behavioral change.

In preparing to use the socio-behavioral approach to alter administrative behavior, the change agent found it necessary to describe more specifically than usual certain behaviors he viewed as having negative consequences for appropriate performance of administrative functions. Examples follow:

1. Lack of punctuality in meeting deadlines: e.g., coming late to work or to meetings, or not completing required reports or complying with special requests.
2. Engaging in such "extraneous" behaviors as making personal telephone calls, and running personal errands during working time.
3. Inappropriate interpersonal behaviors, such as interrupting the work of others, making deals, and soliciting personal consideration.

---

[7] The decline may be attributed to any of several factors—too brief a period of intervention, shifts in the environmental situation, or a reinforcement schedule which was not optimal. Without more complete information, we are of course unable to do more than speculate about this question.

[8] Maxey, *op. cit.*

These represent only a sample of the problems with which the change agent wanted to work. Before starting to work on them, the agent demonstrated how each of these served to interfere with performance on the job.

In carrying out his project the change agent first did an assessment of the behaviors and, by non-intervening observation during a one-week period, established a baseline frequency of occurrence. Intermediate and final goals were set. He then selected the behaviors to reinforce and those to weaken, as well as the intervention techniques to use for these purposes. These were implemented according to the schedule he had developed, monitoring the changes during this period by direct observation. Omitted from the report is any information about alternative sources of reinforcement. This may be because the changes sought were straightforward and simple enough so that the experimenter did not consider the possibility of alternate rewards, or because there did not appear to be any alternate reinforcers available to him.

The intervention reported here deals with the problem of frequent lateness. An analysis of the situation is provided in the following capsule outline of current conditions and proposed intervention.

Baseline information: Subject was late for work three times in five days, without prior approval.

Intermediate objective: Reduce tardiness to two days in five.
Desired goal: Eliminate tardiness without prior approval.
Change techniques:
1. Confront the employee with the rule about tardiness and with the previously-made agreement calling for prior approval of tardiness.
2. Give the employee baseline information on his performance.
3. Monitor his behavior daily, with the employee's knowledge.
4. Whenever the employee is late, call him to the office, make him wait 5-10 minutes in the waiting room, and then confront him with his behavior.

In this instance, the chief technique selected for conscious application was mild punishment. As Thomas and Goodman point out,[9] in punishment one may either present an aversive stimulus or withdraw a positive reinforcer. Change techniques one and four above involve presenting aversive conditions following undesirable behavior. In the first of these, the aversive stimulus is criticism that indicates that the employee has been violating formal rules and also failing to honor a special agreement. In the latter, the aversive stimulus is "inconvenience" (calling him to the office and making him wait) and "unpleasantness" (confronting him with his behavior, saying in effect, "You've been late, and you know you shouldn't be"). The technique of withdrawing a positive reinforcer is illustrated in the explicit use of monitoring, in that its

---

[9] Edwin J. Thomas and Esther Goodman, eds., *Socio-Behavioral Theory and Interpersonal Helping in Social Work* (Ann Arbor: Campus Publisher, 1965), p. 34.

use in this situation removes the positive condition of independence, or the freedom from surveillance favored by professionals and sometimes described as one of the conditions necessary to be considered professional.

Punishment was selected in this situation apparently because the positive reinforcers available to the change agent were not strong enough and also because the punishment was probably seen as easy to administer and unlikely to result in unfavorable side effects. Favorable attention (e.g., praise) was available but was seen as relatively weak, while rewards such as promotion would have been out of proportion. Bonus payments were not available. Whether the gain from the apparent efficiency of the use of punishment instead of positive reinforcement was comparatively greater than the loss due to the possible side effects of punishment, is of course not known here.

Recording of results during intervention showed that during the second week, the late-coming employee was not tardy at all. A brief follow-up undertaken three months after the project's end showed that the employee had continued the punctuality he developed during the project.

Examples of the utilization of behavioral theory in the management of social welfare organizations are of course difficult to produce at this early period in the development of the socio-behavioral approach. However, an example is available from an article by Brethower and Rummler[10] entitled, "For Improved Work Performance: Accentuate the Positive," on the use of learning theory in the management of business and industry. The authors speak of behavioral technology as designed essentially around the concept that "behavior is influenced by its consequences." A clear and simple example which they use to illustrate alteration of factors influencing work behavior follows:

"The people working for Mr. Smith wrote reports that he edited, compiled, and completed in a final report to top management. Every time he put together a final report he found it necessary to telephone his subordinates for additional information and often to have them rewrite their reports. As a result, he always had a crash program on his hands in order to get everything together by the deadline date.

To solve this problem, Smith requested that the men send a file copy of each report they submitted to him. He later returned their file copies with such complimentary notes in the margin as, 'well organized'; 'excellent paragraph'; 'good point'; 'that's the kind of information we can really use.' In short, he accentuated the positive features of each report— and, as a result, he eliminated the negative features. The quality of the

---

[10] Dale M. Brethower and Geary A. Rummler, "For Improved Work Performance: Accentuate the Positive," *Personnel Magazine,* Vol. 43, No. 5 (September/October, 1966), pp. 40-49.

reports rapidly improved. He also found that the men spent more time working on them, so he rarely had to ask for more information."[11]

In this example, Mr. Smith identified the problem behaviors which occurred in the process of preparing reports as long as he followed his usual method. It was easy for him to specify the nature and extent of the change he wanted, because he knew what was needed for the final reports. His intervention consisted essentially of positive reinforcement in the form of complimentary notations on those items of reports Mr. Smith wanted emphasized; the requirement that a file copy be submitted merely made the feedback easier to accomplish.

The examples cited so far illustrate various features common to a socio-behavioral approach to inter-personal problems in administrative practice. Among these are the following:

1. Establishing baselines for behaviors regarded as problematic.
2. Specifying desired ends and states in concrete behavioral terms.
3. Selecting intervention devices described in terms of specific behaviors.
4. Introducing intervention devices.
5. Monitoring behavior to determine the effectiveness of the intervention.
6. Revising the intervention, if necessary, and repeating the cycle indicated above.

BEHAVIOR MODIFICATION BETWEEN ORGANIZATIONS

Just as socio-behavioral techniques have been applied to behavioral change interventions within organizations, it is possible to apply concepts of socio-behavioral theory to change efforts between organizations, or to situations in which one organization seeks to influence another in carrying out functions in which each has some interest. Although the writer is not familiar with any examples from social welfare of attempts to alter with explicit use of socio-behavioral techniques, the behavior of the organization as a system, he can cite a case history of a recent policy effort in public welfare that illustrates aspects of a socio-behavioral approach to change between organizations.

In 1960, the Commissioner of Social Security in the U.S. Department of Health, Education, and Welfare held a hearing to determine whether the State of Louisiana was not in conformity with the Social Security Act because of its passage that year of a law concerning the Aid to Dependent Children program. The feature the Commissioner viewed as problematic was the "suitable home" provision, which he considered to impose an irrelevant eligibility condition for the receipt of assistance. The most extreme sanction available to the federal government was the withholding of federal matching

---

[11] *Ibid.,* p. 44.

funds. Simply holding a hearing would have constituted a threat of this action. The threat of a hearing, in turn, would be an aversive stimulus, with the intent to suppress the undesirable behavior.

The so-called controlling conditions for the offensive clause were considered by many people to be (1) the tense state of race relations in Louisiana, where Negro families made up a considerable proportion of the ADC caseload; (2) a general "anti-welfare" attitude which, in many states, receives occasional expression in the enactment of restrictive welfare laws; and (3) the opinion of many states that the Department of Health, Education, and Welfare would not utilize its option to withhold funds, but rather would only express the judgment that the requirement was unsound from a "policy" point of view.

The specific "behavior" which the Commissioner sought to change was the implementation of a state law that would have undesirable consequences for many children. This change would mean reinstatement to ADC of some 23,000 children, and discontinuance of the eligibility requirement at issue. The desired change, in fact, included not only the two results just mentioned, but also the state's not utilizing other criteria to achieve the same undesirable result.

The Commissioner of Social Security was performing functionally in the capacity of rule-enforcer. Non-compliance with his directive would have produced failure to reinforce the state's action, in the form of withdrawal of federal funds. The threat of a hearing, with the attendant publicity and negotiations, served, on the basis of prior experience, as an aversive condition, which might be mild or severe, depending upon past history regarding the use of this threat and similar ones. The threat of a hearing served also as a discriminative stimulus in that it alerted the state agency to the likelihood of non-reinforcement of prior behavior if that behavior was continued.

The aversiveness of the threats turned out to be too mild, and finally it was necessary for the Secretary of Health, Education, and Welfare, Arthur Flemming, to issue a ruling to make clear the federal position in this matter.[12] In the analytic framework used here, the ruling was another discriminative stimulus—apparently a much stronger one. Further changes in state law and practice was subsequently made. There was public compliance; a state agency had been changed. But immediate and substantial change in actual discriminatory practices probably did not occur,[13] for the informal norms and traditions relating to such practices had not been otherwise affected.

---

[12] "Effective July 1, 1961, a state plan . . . may not impose an eligibility condition that would deny assistance with respect to a needy child on the basis that the home conditions in which the child lives are unsuitable, while the child continues to reside in the home." Bureau of Publc Assistance, Department of Health, Education and Welfare, *State Letter No. 452* (January 17, 1961) mimeo., p. 1.

[13] For comprehensive discussion of this situation see Winifred Bell, *Aid to Dependent Children* (New York: Columbia University Press, 1965), especially pp. 137-151.

DISCUSSION

Socio-behavioral theory contributes to administrative practice a focus on the need for specificity in defining problematic behavior and controlling conditions, in establishing change goals and intervention strategies, and in measuring outcomes. It clarifies the importance of a demonstrable relationship between rewards and desired behaviors; and calls attention to the availability of reinforcers in the form of devices used for other purposes (e.g., note taking and other forms of recording) and such common reinforcers as approval and attention that can be manipulated simply and directly through personal interaction.

Furthermore, if we desire to foster some kinds of behavior in our organizations and to minimize others, we will need to analyze carefully the kinds of behavior exhibited by those who serve as models. For example, consider the executive as a model. Many people have had the experience of being participants in a staff meeting considered by the head of the agency to be important enough so that he himself attends as a means of indicating its significance. But most executives are busy people, much sought after and preoccupied with many matters. This condition means that they sometimes think about other matters while at meetings, or are called out to take care of something requiring their immediate attention, with the result that an executive may be entering and leaving meetings frequently and at odd times. This behavior is not exemplary of conduct the executive would want imitated by employees. If the executive wishes to show the meeting's importance and to serve as a better model, he should either attend faithfully and pay attention, or not appear at all and have the reasons for non-attendance clearly understood.

Socio-behavioral theory also directs attention to the types, magnitudes, and schedules of reinforcement operative in organizations. For example, consider the formal and informal system of contingencies for work performance. Despite gradual development of merit system policies and practices in social welfare organizations, there is, in general, no clearly identifiable relationship between salary and other benefits and the performance of desired behavior. Thus, the use of immediate monetary rewards would require substantial alteration of most personnel policies. It is also the case that many administrators are more likely to utilize punishment than rewards in dealing with employees. Also, in many cases a major stumbling block in producing behavior change is the fact that the new behavior may produce aversive consequences in the microsystem of which the employee is a part. Many reinforcement systems are at work on a welfare worker. For example, he may please his superior by seeing more clients or by processing more cases, but this may elicit the wrath of his co-workers. Work performance is typically under control of many *immediate* reinforcers. The microcosm in which the person works is very often actually more potent than the larger system, because this informal system has

68

its own norms that are frequently implemented by string contingencies immediately dispensed for conforming and non-conforming behavior.

Socio-behavioral practice rests on at least two important assumptions. The first is that one can describe a behavior or procedure that raises the functioning level of the administrative operation; and the second is that an effective "reward-punishment-model" regimen may be defined and applied.

The first assumption requires that some agreement be reached on goals among the organizational participants and that "deviant" or impeding behavior, because of personal goals incompatible with the objectives of the administrative unit as a whole, not appear. In our case examples, this assumption would be violated if, for example, the following were true:

> Example 1 (the committee, page 60): The source of reward in the group and the motivation for participating were to socialize, kibitz, and "take pot shots" at the staff.

> Example 2 (the latecomer, page 63): The non-work obligations were more potent and important than those of work.

> Example 3 (writing reports, page 65): The report writer was dissatisfied with his performance or his job and incomplete reports would allow him to avoid unfavorable evaluation which, in turn, might lead to depression or even resignation.

When such deviant, personal goals occur and are in conflict with those of the organization, efforts will probably have to be diverted toward establishing and strengthening a consensus on desirable goals for the organization and the individuals in it.

The second assumption is not met if the administrator does not have available the requisite rewards and punishments. Clearly, the reinforcements must be available and strong enough to compete successfully with others which currently support the behavior to be changed. Behavioral change applications typically occur within the context of a larger system. Change may well require adding to a particular aspect of the administrative situation interventions (such as rewards, punishments, models), independent of the existing reward structure, so that new behaviors may be shaped and generalized. For substantial and lasting change to occur, it is frequently necessary to alter the general reward structure, and this requires that careful attention be paid to the entire system that is the context for performance in the organization.

POSTSCRIPT

In this paper, socio-behavioral theory has been used to describe and explain administrative behavior. An attempt has also been made to suggest that it can serve for planning administrative efforts. Among its advantages is the focused emphasis on the necessity of establishing objectives and sub-objectives defined in terms of specific, achievable, and measurable behaviors—an emphasis much needed in social work administration as well as in other fields. Similarly, this approach fosters a critical examination of the specific rewards and punishments that have been built up in large-scale personnel systems, generally, and in social welfare organizations, in particular.

The emphases of the socio-behavioral approach to administration are similar to at least some of those contained in other contemporary viewpoints (e.g., systems analysis). Further explorations of the utility of socio-behavioral theory for purposes such as those examined in this paper should probably be undertaken with special attention to the relationship between its assumptions and those of other theories concerned with organizational behavior.

Discussion

Question 1. The paper gave the impression that reward and punishment are interchangeable. Isn't it true that sometimes punishment can reinforce?

*Rothman.** That interpretation would be incorrect. Dr. Lind was not using them interchangeably. He was using them differentially. Professor Lind used another example in which an attempt was made to have a person at a staff meeting speak more frequently. This man was an under-participant at meetings. What was done was that every time he spoke, the supervisor turned to him, smiled, nodded his head, and later made favorable comments. There was the conscious application of reward in that situation. In this other situation, the same supervisor used mainly punishment. He was using them differentially.

Question 2. He pointed out, however, that he couldn't offer a strong enough reward. Are they interchangeable?

Thomas. They're not. This gets into some technical details on which I will comment briefly. Positive reinforcement is used to strengthen behavior and to maintain behavior. Punishment, in the sense of applying an aversive stimulus following response, or in the sense of withdrawing a positive reinforcer following a response, is almost always *not* used to strengthen behavior or to maintain behavior. Rather, it is used to weaken behavior, or in some cases, to eliminate it. That's a very important distinction. Furthermore, negative reinforcement (that is, the withdrawal of an aversive condition following a response) which was included in the example involving lateness, presupposes the presentation of an aversive condition at the outset. Something aversive cannot be removed unless it first has been made present. This oftentimes leads to some difficulties. Actually, behaviorally speaking, presentation of an aversive condition following a response, or prior to a response, has different behavioral effects as compared to the removal of the aversive condition following a response. The latter, the removal of an aversive condition following a response, is a negative reinforcing operation, to use the language more exactly. Presentation of an aversive stimulus following a response is a punishing operation. The operations are different; the consequences are different.

---

* Because Dr. Lind could not attend the Conference, his paper was read by a colleague, Dr. Rothman.

71

Question 3. Could you define "What is a unit of behavior?" and secondly, "What are the criteria for the selection of behavior among many selections which you might have?"

Thomas. What is a unit of behavior? You are asking this in general? That is a very interesting question. I would like to speak practically on this. The unit of behavior is going to be those subresponses, generally more than one response, defined as problematic and having similar controlling conditions. Theoretically, a unit of behavior is very difficult to talk about, although in this theoretical tradition they talk about the operant which is the class of responses which has a fuctionally similar consequence in the contingency system of the environment. There may be various ways, for example, in which you could express disagreement. The operant consists perhaps of that entire class of responses which brings about the same environmental consequences. One of the profound implications of the notion of operant is that we get away from the details of miniscule response. Whatever the unit of behavior, however, it is necessary to be behaviorally specific concerning exactly what it is we wish to change and the conditions that control it.

Question 4. What are your criteria of selection?

Thomas. You are asking what the criteria are for defining a problematic social response. What are the criteria for defining deviance? All I have to say is that we have to concern ourselves with the norms of the social system in which we live. We do not talk about inherent pathologies and the like, except where they can be demonstrated organically. We are dealing with social conventions concerning that which is regarded as atypical, abnormal, or deviant. Now that gets us into what those social definitions are, and I think that such a discussion would take us too far afield.

V.
IMPLICATIONS OF THE SOCIO-BEHAVIORAL APPROACH FOR COMMUNITY ORGANIZATION PRACTICE

Phillip Fellin
Jack Rothman
Henry J. Meyer

The purpose of this paper is to explore some implications of the socio-behavioral approach for community organization practice. This approach stresses behavioral specificity and control in its practice and operationality and empirical support for the knowledge it uses. Thus, where theories of community organization practice have been vague, concepts philosophical or non-operational, and intervention goals and methods global, the perspective of socio-behavioral theory can be expected to have a desirable influence. Where community organization practice has been essentially non-theoretical and experiential, it may benefit from the stress of socio-behavioral theory on implementing variables, the effectiveness of which has been empirically demonstrated.

The development of the socio-behavioral approach for individual and group levels of intervention has served as an impetus for considering this approach for community organization practice.[1] However, the knowledge and practice techniques developed for one level of phenomena cannot be substituted at other levels. Hence, present efforts will be directed toward examination of the requisites of socio-behavioral practice in relation to community organization practice. The authors are not aware of previous attempts to relate

---

[1] See Edwin J. Thomas and Esther Goodman, eds., *Socio-Behavioral Theory and Interpersonal Helping in Social Work* (Ann Arbor: Campus Publishers, 1965).

the socio-behavioral approach to community organization. Therefore, this is an exploratory and illustrative paper, rather than a report based on systematic study and practice experience.

MAJOR THEMES OF PRACTICE

The socio-behavioral approach identifies at least five major themes having to do with behavioral specification of practice activities relevant to achieving stabilization and change.[2] The first theme of sociol-behavioral practice emphasizes the behavioral specification of problematic behavior. Attempts to meet this practice requirement on the community level are illustrated in the Mobilization for Youth Project of New York City.[3] Having as a goal the reduction of juvenile delinquency, Mobilization for Youth sought to discover the nature of local juvenile behavior by taking into account newspaper reports; perceptions of area residents; information from gang members, from social agencies, and from official police and court data. For example, when residents of the area ranked problems such as those relating to the public schools, transportation, city police protection, teen-agers' behavior, and behavior of certain racial groups, it was found that teen-age behavior was identified by 64.5 percent of the sample of 988 adults as the largest or next largest problem.[4] Specific behaviors, such as using dope, stealing, and drinking, were also evaluated by the residents in terms of how serious they thought they were.

Further specification of problematic behaviors was required by the Project because slum neighborhood delinquency was viewed as caused by lack of opportunity for upward social mobility, and the Project program emphasized "changing the environment" rather than "changing individuals."[5] The Project, therefore, attempted specification of problematic community conditions and behaviors, such as lack of job opportunity, racial barriers to mobility, and lack of organizational affiliations and neighborhood ties. In order to obtain this information, a survey questionnaire was administered to a random sample of residents in the target area and to staff (both professional and non-professional) employed to work with the residents.

These efforts at problem specification have the common feature of ascertaining the social definition of the behaviors thought to be problematic by the

---

[2] Edwin J. Thomas, "The Socio-Behavioral Approach: Illustrations and Analysis," pp. 11-15.

[3] Mobilization for Youh, Inc., *A Proposal for the Prevention and Control of Delinquency by Expanding Opportunities* (New York: Mobilization for Youth, Inc., 1961).

[4] *Ibid.*, p. 4.

[5] Bertram M. Beck, "A (New) Social Work Model," *Social Service Review,* Vol. 40, No. 3 (September, 1966), p. 270.

staff and the clients. But for purposes of practice, even further specification of the behaviors would be indicated. The exact nature of gaps in services was revealed through a survey of such social resources as schools, recreation programs, public and private social agencies, churches and voluntary associations.

A second theme of socio-behavioral practice involves the specification of controlling conditions in regard to problematic behaviors. The Mobilization for Youth Project called for "close examination of the conditions under which various forms of delinquency emerge."[6] There was concern with the characteristics of the social structure associated with such major types of gangs as the criminal, conflict, and retreatist. The Project noted that the nature of the social integration of slum communities (organized vs. unorganized) is an identifiable characteristic of community structure, that restricts or reinforces the particular content of delinquent behavior. For example, in the case of the conflict subculture, conditions in the contemporaneous environment that bring about an unintegrated community can be identified and evaluated in terms of their influence on the conflict solution. These conditions include high rates of mobility, changing land use, lack of legitimate channels for success, and absence of effective patterns of social control.

A third requirement for socio-behavioral practice is the specific and behavioral definition of change goals. On the community level, this approach leads to the specification of goals in terms of concrete changes sought in the community. Thus the meaning of "changing the community" becomes specified in terms of the patterns of behavior that may be altered. In regard to exchange relationships between social agencies, the use of agency services in the community, and the development of new organizations, exact behaviors to be changed need to be specified in the statement of goals. Such specifications might include a given number of people who use an agency service; a certain increase in the exchange of information between such organizations as the school, the juvenile court, and the welfare department, when they have a client in common; a specified decrease in the unemployment rate for a particular age, educational level, or ethnic group in the community; or an exact increase in local organizations in which the poor participate. These usually have been referred to by community organization practitioners as "task" goals. Goals identified in practice as "process" goals are also subject to identification in specific, behavioral terms. For example, consider as illustrative here the number of people who participate in voluntary associations, the number of contacts between people of different racial or social class levels, and the number of the poor participating in decision-making.

The call for goal development in specific, behavioral terms can be found in some of the current community organization literature and practices. For example, Morris and Binstock recommend explicit goal statements, where the

---

[6] Mobilization for Youth, *op. cit.*, p. 77.

"planner's preferences become embodied in a series of relatively concrete objectives."[7] Another example comes from the work of Alinsky in which he stresses defining specific issues which people can crystallize as a foundation for their change attempts. This focus on identification and specification of goals in behavioral, operational terms, however, is in contrast to such global goals as "increasing community cohesion" found in some circles of social welfare planning and community development.

Specification of goals also involves the ordering of intermediate goals in relationship to final goals. For example, Ross considers short- and long-term targets in community organization practice, especially in situations where it is not possible to reach major objectives immediately and where the attainment of sub-goals provides immediate rewards which sustain interest and commitment to long-range objectives.[8] The fully specified ordering of operations goals is a "behavioral curriculum."

Having identified practice goals dealing with the change or stabilization of behavior at the community level, the task remains to state the techniques of intervention in concrete, functionally specific terms, and to relate given strategies to these specific goals. In this context, consider the proposal of the Mobilization for Youth Project for limiting conflict behavior by focusing on changing the community. General strategies for change included "building patterns of relationships among adults," "strengthening indigenous institutional forms in the community," "increasing capacity to impose informal sanctions."[9] In operational terms, this means employing various techniques to stimulate lower-class slum residents to participate in local neighborhood activities. For example, one technique involved the development of new types of organizations, such as a League of Store-Front Churches, which then could dramatize the needs of area residents, and increase communication between residents and local social institutions. A second illustration of a change strategy concerns efforts to tap into the informal network of social relations in the area. A "Starter Program" was proposed by Mobilization for Youth which involved recruiting and training indigenous leaders in the community. Opinion leaders in the community are identified, and various approaches are used to bring about attendance and assessment of the leaders in relation to the tasks defined as problematic by staff and resident. One such task might involve organization of the unaffiliated; another might involve helping newcomers in their assimilation into the community, with the community organizer serving as a detached expert to interpret community resources as well as to facilitate community involvement.

---

[7] Robert Morris and Robert H. Binstock, *Feasible Planning for Social Change* (New York: Columbia University Press, 1960), p. 89.

[8] Murray G. Ross, *Community Organization* (New York: Harper and Brothers, 1955), p. 189.

[9] Mobilization for Youth, *op. cit.,* p. 88.

One of the features of these illustrations of change strategies is the lack of conceptualization and terminology for describing them. Many of the related techniques are still insufficiently operationally and behaviorally specific. In a later section of this paper, various concrete ways to achieve linkage between primary groups and formal organizations are systematically discussed. In all cases, the socio-behavioral approach requires further specification of what the community organization practitioner actually does in carrying out his general strategy of change.

A fifth feature of socio-behavioral practice involves the behavioral specification of outcomes. This operation allows for evaluation of the change efforts in terms of anticipated as well as unanticipated outcomes. It requires systematic documentation of interventional activities and outcomes, with procedures for collection, recording, and analysis of relevant data. In this way, intervention can be evaluated in terms of the conditions under which it succeeds or fails. This type of assessment depends largely upon exact behavioral specification of outcomes, and, in addition, on having the means to monitor the outcomes. For example, in a situation where techniques are used to obtain attendance, a system for reliably recording attendance would, of course, be necessary, as would additional information about the reasons for non-attendance in the program.

These characteristics of socio-behavioral practice provide significant guidelines for change-oriented practice at the community level. Illustrations have been presented to offer a grasp of the requisites for community organization practice based on a socio-behavioral framework. The themes discussed here may not seem altogether new to many community organization practitioners. Both the literature and practice experience have called upon the practitioner to be clear about causal factors in problem situations and specific about projected goals. A socio-behavioral perspective, however, compels application that is more systematic, comprehensive, deliberate, and rigorous than is the general mode of practice. In the next section, the socio-behavioral approach is more fully considered in relation to one area of community organization practice, i.e., ways in which practitioners seek to link primary groups and formal organization. The "linking mechanisms" advanced are viewed as empirically derived, natural points of accessibility between and among community units, and are, therefore, socio-behavioral in nature.

INTERORGANIZATIONAL LINKAGE AND THE SOCIO-BEHAVIORAL APPROACH

Community organization practice refers to change efforts by social workers at the community level with relevance to such activities as organizing new services and bringing new resources into the community, coordinating and maximizing delivery systems of services, changing aspects of community structure that are inimical to social welfare, promoting community cohesion, and developing community competence in problem-solving. The community serves as both a context and a target in this method of practice. While the community is, in the world of reality, a complex and fluid social configuration, it is useful, from the standpoint of analysis and practice, to select from the various structures and processes composing the community certain variables which are considered to be functionally important, accessible and manipulable. Two fundamental social units in most contemporary communities are primary groups and formal organizations. Thus a community may be viewed analytically in terms of the types and numbers of primary groups and formal organizations that exist and their patterns of interrelationship. Practice can be viewed in terms of behavioral modifications that are necessary in the linkage patterns between these social units in order to promote given social welfare goals.

Possible interrelationships between the units identified include: primary groups to primary groups, primary groups to formal organizations, formal organizations to primary groups, and formal organizations to formal organizations. Each of these possibilities involves different variables and suggests different modes of practice. Thus, a mandate to be behaviorally specific necessitates treatment of each set of linkages.

The concentration here is on linkages between formal organizations and primary groups. Assumptions relating to the practice aspects of manipulating such linkages may be briefly reviewed. In a complex industrial society, formal organizations play a highly significant role because of their possession of such resources as professional-technical expertise, manpower, money, facilities, and information. Thus, formal organizations in the social welfare field have a great deal to contribute to community well-being and problem-solving. But primary groups are important also because of their socio-emotional supports to the individual, and their ability to endure over time and to react quickly to on-the-spot emergencies. The formal organization is equipped to deal with fairly uniform repetitive and rationally conceived tasks, whereas the primary group is best adapted to deal with non-uniform, idiosyncratic and emotionally relevant tasks.

While formal organizations and primary groups make different contributions in pursuing social welfare goals, their separate impacts can be reinforcing and complementary. In pursuing their goals, formal organizations can maximize their efforts by linking with primary groups that can play a complementary role in achieving these goals. To be most effective, such a linkage should strike a point of balance, i.e., bring the two social units close enough together to reinforce each other, but not so close that they contaminate and cripple one another.[10] In their review of practice and social science literature,

---

[10] Eugene Litwak and Henry J. Meyer, "A Balance Theory of Coordination Between Bureaucratic Organizations and Community Primary Groups," *Administrative Science Quarterly,* Vol. 11, No. 1 (June, 1966), pp. 31-58.

Litwak and Meyer have isolated a number of means by which formal organizations typically achieve contact with primary groups. This set of linking mechanisms is described below:

1. *The detached worker:* Use of a professional person who enters the primary group (e.g., a family, neighborhood club) and, through a trusting, quasi-primary group relationship, attempts to change specific attitudes and behaviors. (Example: street worker with delinquent gangs.)
2. *Opinion leader:* Use by a professional person from the organization of natural, indigenous leaders to affect, in specific terms, groups over which the opinion leader has influence.
3. *Settlement house:* Use of physical facilities and professional persons in the home territory of primary groups to achieve specific behavior changes. (Examples: store-front recreation programs, adult education programs in neighborhood schools.)
4. *Voluntary associations:* Use of a voluntary association to bring together professionals from the formal organization and members of local primary groups so that change efforts can be attempted. (Example: PTA.)
5. *Common messenger:* Use of common members of both the formal organization and primary groups to transmit specific types of communications. (Example: Child brings messages from school to the family.)
6. *Mass media:* Use by the formal organization of media of public communication to influence primary groups. (Example: Use of newspapers, television, flyers, posters.)
7. *Formal authority:* Use of legal authority or well-established informal authority to require primary group members to conform with given expectations. (Example: Attendance officer compelling the family to send a child to school.)
8. *Delegated function:* Use by the formal organization of another organization that has authority or influence over the primary group. (Example: The school requests that the police deal with the family concerning a behavior problem.)

Certain criteria have been proposed by Litwak and Meyer for applying these mechanisms in practice.[11] These criteria include the variables of intensity, initiative, focused expertise, and scope. Certain mechanisms have great initiative and intensity (such as the detached expert); others have great scope (mass media, common messenger). Generally speaking, the greater the distance between the goals of the formal organization and the receptivity of the primary

---

[11] Litwak and Meyer, *op. cit.,* pp. 39ff.

group, the greater the need to use mechanisms possessing initiative and intensity. The more complex the immediate problem, the greater the need to use mechanisms involving focused expertise.

To illustrate the socio-behavioral requirement for specificity and the use of linking mechanisms, the problems of furthering educational goals through the institution of the school is presented. The specific practice problem is to seek out means by which schools can improve educational performance, particularly in the case of children residing in culturally deprived homes and neighborhoods. It is obvious that the family and neighborhood primary groups are highly relevant in influencing educational motivation. The question is how the school may link with such primary groups in order to move the groups toward constructively supporting educational objectives. Accordingly, the area of community organization practice emphasized is the provision of services by formal organizations to primary groups. The ultimate goal is improved educational performance. This can be measured concretely through test scores in a number of educational testing devices, both verbal and nonverbal. A series of intermediate, instrumental goals would need to be established. These goals might include having parents help children with their homework, having parents bring more books into the home, helping parents deal with behavior problems of children (that militate against educational goals), and raising the educational level and aspirations of parents through their participation in voluntary associations and adult education classes. These intermediate goals can be concretized on the same basis as long-range goals, and the effectiveness of various linking mechanisms in attaining these middle-range goals may be assessed for the different population groups involved.

A simple and delimited goal such as bringing more books into the home by the parents might involve use of mechanisms such as the mass media, settlement house and common messenger. The school might buy books in bulk quantities and sell them to parents at reduced cost. Announcements in the newspapers or in a house-organ-type of newsletter, emphasizing savings, might be sufficient to stimulate some parents to purchase additional books. Or, in the settlement-house approach, an attractive display might be set up in the lobby of the school or in some central location where adult education classes are held. Having staff available at display tables could then serve the purpose of pointing out to parents gains to the child and the family, as well as savings or status factors. The common messenger mechanisms could be employed through encouraging the child to urge his parents to bring home more books. The child might receive a reward—gold star or extra privileges—for every "x" number of new books acquired in the home.

Aiding parents in dealing with behavior problems of children is a more complicated undertaking and might require use of mechanisms involving greater intensity, such as the detached worker or delegated function. The detached worker can go out to the family in its home environment and provide

80

knowledge and guidance on the spot, with much concentration and over a substantial period of time. In the problem under consideration, the practitioner would need to communicate knowledge concerning developmental psychology, techniques of child rearing as well as societal values concerning acceptable child or parent behavior. In using this mechanism, there can be immediate feedback, modeling behavior by the practitioner, and sustained reinforcement and support. But, should the worker lack the skills or time necessary to work with a particular family or neighborhood group as a detached worker, he might evoke the delegated function mechanism by referring the family or group to another source of help. In the instance under discussion, he might refer the parent to a child guidance clinic or a family service agency, or the child to the "Y." Sometimes it may be necessary to couple these mechanisms in a phased sequence, as suggested above, using initially the detached worker mechanism as a means of preparing the family to accept the delegated function mechanism.[12]

This examination of selected approaches to effecting change in patterns between families and schools illustrates aspects of socio-behavioral practice at the community level. The focus on linking mechanisms reflects one requisite of socio-behavioral knowledge, i.e., direct relevance of the knowledge to problems of change. Furthermore, knowledge about the linking mechanisms has considerable empirical support, particularly through practice experience. Also, the knowledge is operational, in that the concepts are identifiable, accessible, and manipulable. Further development and refinement of this type of substantive knowledge for socio-behavioral practice at the community level is indicated. This will require identification and formulation of generalizations about change pertinent to the community. The implementation of the knowledge can then be guided along the lines indicated in the themes of socio-behavioral practice.

COMMUNITY ORGANIZATION
AND INTERPERSONAL CHANGE

In conjunction with the community organization practitioner's involvement in change at the community level, he frequently seeks behavioral change on an interpersonal level. For this purpose, he may draw upon substantive socio-behavioral knowledge and practice experience that pertains to this level of

---

[12] We have not gone into detail in regard to specific worker activities and modes of influence in using these mechanisms. Further development along these lines occurs in a comprehensive manual currently being employed in the Community Organization Program at The University of Michigan School of Social Work. See Eugene Litwak et al., *Theory and Practice of School-Community Relationships: A Manual,* The University of Michigan School of Social Work, 1966, mimeographed.

intervention. Thus, in his work with committees and task-oriented groups, the practitioner often seeks to eliminate maladaptive behaviors by individuals that inhibit group goals and to produce new behaviors. For such situations, established socio-behavioral techniques may be applicable for teaching skills to individuals and groups, identifying and handling problems, and creating and maintaining group norms to allow for productive use of committee meetings. Some socio-behavioral techniques that have been adapted from learning theory include reinforcement and shaping, extinction, discrimination, punishment, and imitative modeling. When these methods are employed by the community organization practitioner to bring about interpersonal change, the change is sought for instrumental purposes, i.e., as a step in a more general plan to effect change on the community level. The group or committee becomes the instrument through which broader and more salient change takes place. The focus of intervention is on change of maladaptive behavior or the acquisition of new behaviors in order to achieve community objectives.

Some techniques for helping individuals acquire new patterns of behavior are particularly appropriate in community organization. Thus, techniques such as model presentation, role modeling, and identification may be used in work with several target groups of current practice, e.g., in developing leadership in low income areas, or in developing communication skills for individuals with low formal educational achievements. Various aspects of modeling, examined in behavioral literature, are applicable to community organization, such as Kanfer's discussion of "vicarious human reinforcements."[13] This approach involves the client's observation of the successful execution of some behavior by a model. Bandura adds an important modeling dimension in his consideration of "no trial learning," where he notes that in situations such as teaching adults vocational skills, "the behavior of models is utilized extensively to accelerate the acquisition process."[14] The individual learns from watching the behaviors of the real-life model, who may be observed handling a variety of problem-solving situations, and whose behavior may be imitated. An example within community organization practice involving modeling would be a situation where the practitioner, working with a voluntary association, carries out the role of chairman of the group until a member learns the behaviors appropriate to the position. Group members may also observe the practitioner representing the group in meetings or contacts with representatives of other groups. This technique may also be employed to develop indigenous leaders, who in turn serve as models for group members. Coaching, which requires a natural "real life" setting, is still another technique that appears to be particu-

---

[13] Frederick H. Kanfer, "Vicarious Human Reinforcements: A Glimpse Into the Black Box," in Leonard Krasner and Leonard Ullmann, eds., *Research in Behavior Modification* (New York: Holt, Rinehart and Winston, 1965), p. 267.

[14] Albert Bandura, "Behavior Modifications Through Modeling Procedures," in Krasner and Ullmann, *op. cit.,* p. 312.

larly adaptable to community organization, especially where the practitioner works directly with persons in the course of their normal participation in civic affairs.

The use of socio-behavioral approaches to bring about interpersonal change has had limited development in practice. As with all interpersonal technologies of change, questions remain as to the extent to which the practitioner can control selected factors that affect particular individual or community behaviors. Also, it is important when working at the interpersonal level to determine the relevance of the interventions to objectives at the community level.

CONCLUSION

The socio-behavioral approach has at least two significant implications for community organization practice. First, the approach reinforces a general change-oriented perspective useful for community organization practice through its major themes and its emphasis on rationalistic approaches to change. Secondly, substantive knowledge of socio-behavioral theory and methods of change at the interpersonal level may be assimilated and utilized by the community organization practitioner. Precautions should be taken, however, to not make knowledge and practice on the interpersonal level automatically analogous to that required on the community level. The need remains for the development of socio-behavioral knowledge at the community level (e.g., propositions about the ways in which a community functions, and identification of crucial environmental variables involved in change operations). While the socio-behavioral approach offers a useful perspective for those engaged in community organization practice, it has yet to be applied in a systematic way in this area of social work. The examination of socio-behavioral theory in relation to community organization practice suggests one avenue for further exploration, application, and evaluation that will serve as a prologue to the development of more and better theory on the community level.

Discussion

Question 1. I have a problem distinguishing between change of an individual and the change of systems. Can this approach be used to change entire systems rather than some of the individuals in the system?

Rothman. The socio-behavioral perspective can be applied to systems, just as it can be applied to individuals. In the "Mobilization for Youth" example, this was illustrated. Changes were aimed at certain institutions and how they were to function. These changes in institutions, say the schools, made the school sysem work more effectively to provide opportunities to low-income kids. One could approach this on a socio-behavioral basis. Change the institution and then have the institution have a broad effect on the community.

Question 2. You say that socio-behavioral theory was used to change the school system. You link the parents with the system. What are some of the specific techniques used in relation with the school system?

Rothman. In this paper, the point was made that we're bringing the perspective of socio-behaviorial theory to community organization, not the specific techniques that have been worked out in terms of individual change.

Sarri. We discussed structural changes in social systems. These changes can be behaviorally specific. However, one cannot expect the same interpersonal level concepts to be used at the social system level, because there we are talking about systems, not individuals. Systems cannot be understood as collections of individuals or just aggregates; because they *are* systems they must be analyzed and dealt with as systems.

Question 3. One of the papers mentioned that a tape recorder was used to reinforce norms.

Sarri. That is a situation in which we are trying to change individuals and norms. To change systems, we change structures, the ways and conditions under which people can interact and exchange. Such change cannot be achieved solely by changing individuals. For example, if you wished to change the opportunities for people to participate, you would create a structural change so that they could see each other more often—say daily rather than once a week. In the school system, for instance, you can change the pattern of exchange between teachers, special education staff, and parents. This is a structural change. It is distinct from changing those individuals who are engaged in the enterprise.

Comment 4. Along this line, you will not persuade a school bo𝑎
intendent and his staff to try some new structural change (or so
tice) unless you can show them that they may get some goals 𝑎
fully by new procedures than by the old. If they try something
not going to repeat it unless they get more reinforcement that 𝗏
the meaning of reinforcement perhaps is more complicated as
system.

Sarri. You are referring to attainment of organizational goals.
understand reinforcement for the individual merely as one way t𝗈
for the organization. A school system, for example, may have a 𝖼
of 30 percent. Suppose it is able to reduce this rate to 15 perc𝖾
more effectively attain some other goals. A superintendent himsel
inforced because his organization is doing better, but these two t
not be understood as identical. Reinforcement for the superin𝗍
consequence of attaining the organizational goal.

Question 5. I would be interested to know whether applications
proach have been made when problematic behavior happens to be
with high status in the power structure.

How would you use this approach in a community organizati𝗈
such as a rent strike against landlords, where the activities on the
group are to bring about changes in high-status persons? I can s
clearly when the worker is lined up with, rather than against, the p

Sarri. One of the things one must determine about power is wh
social power is at issue in a given situation. Did the situation in
expert or legitimate power? You want to make an analytical distin𝖼
and then decide on a particular approach or strategy for that particul
power. I don't think the high-status person necessarily required 𝑎
socio-behavioral approach than the low-status person. It is necessary
these particular problematic behavior situations and then to handl𝖾
its own terms.

Thomas. I'd like to make a comment. It is a very good point that
ciple, it doesn't matter about status, but in practice if you are deali𝗇
high power person, he may have more power than you have. One of
important implications of stressing controlling conditions and the alt𝖾
the contingencies of the environment to bring about change is that 𝗒
have the power to "win." If there is nothing you can do about this
that's that! You have been beaten, so to speak.

Another implication is that if you focus upon these external co
conditions as being among the most viable factors in bringing about 𝗆

ion, then it follows that for certain proper objectives we would wish to extend the legitimate domain of control because, otherwise, plans will fail quite regularly and nothing will happen. Without proper control, we will just worry about things (like housing) and talk about them, but nothing will be achieved.

Sarri. I think Dr. Fellin would agree that some of the experiences at the community level that proceed with a behavioral approach have been remarkably successful in obtaining some important goals. Rent strikes, for example, have worked in some places, and they have proceeded with distinct behavioral plans.

Question 6. Does this involve conflict theory?

Thomas. No, this is not necessarily conflict theory. However, conflict looks like one of the more promising existing theories. That is, conflict theory in the community context appears to contain some generalizations and practice procedures that qualify as being socio-behavioral substance at the community level.

Question 7. May I ask Fellin if in his work in the community he has applied this approach to change of total organizations in contrast to changes in individuals in organizations. For instance, has there been the effort at changing total schools, either specific schools or total school systems, or have you just been focusing on some of the behavior of some of the students and some of the families?

Fellin. We should make clear that at the community level we have been mainly exploring the promise of the socio-behavioral approach. However, some of the students are actually engaged in using some mechanisms and change strategies in work with organizations and individuals.

Question 8. Has anyone in your group or elsewhere tried to take a low-quality elementary school and change its quality?

Sarri. There have been several experiments.

Thomas. There are reports indicating that the level of academic performance of young men in a prison-type situation has been dramatically raised by behavioral methods.

Sarri. The Cohen experiment at the National Training School in Washington, D. C. demonstrated remarkable change in education level. There are also reports on such efforts in regular public elementary schools.

VI.
ORGANIZATIONAL REQUISITES FOR A SOCIO-BEHAVIORAL TECHNOLOGY

Rosemary C. Sarri
Robert D. Vinter

S ocial influence methodologies of central concern to social work are conducted in and through agencies and other service organizations. Each methodology poses its own demands for agency arrangements, and each presents a distinctive configuration of requirements for effective implementation. It is no less true that service agencies, as organizations, shape and constrain the various technologies they embody, and that the functional requirements of an organization are never simply those defined by one or another technology. Aspects of this reciprocal relation will be examined here and the particular demands posed for organizations by socio-behavioral technology will be considered. In doing so, concentration will be on direct-service agencies that are primarily concerned with individual clients, but much said also has relevance to community practice and other organizations. Analysis is necessarily limited both by the extent to which those reporting socio-behavioral practice have discussed its organizational aspects, and because such practice is very much in an emerging phase.

THE HUMAN SERVICE ORGANIZATION

The perspective of this paper on social agencies as "human service" organizations initiates the discussion. Such organizations consist of community agencies for welfare, education, and social control that are mandated by society, some for the socialization of individuals so that they will be prepared to per-

87

form social roles adequately, and others for the treatment and resocialization of persons who are not adequately performing conventional social roles.[1] These units process individuals into new statuses, and utilize human relations technologies to reduce deviant behavior and to assist individuals in the acquisition of acceptable modes of behavior. Included in this range of organizations are mental hospitals and clinics, prisons, public welfare agencies, juvenile courts, family service and children's agencies, public schools, and agencies for the physically handicapped and retarded.

Social welfare agencies must be viewed both as administrative bureaucracies and as social systems.[2] They are administrative bureaucracies in that they are established to attain specific goals, and their internal structures, technologies and procedures are designed to implement these goals. The particular nature of an agency's goals serves to define relationships between itself and its social environment; they influence the choice of technologies and staff personnel; and they guide the coordination of organizational members. Agencies are thus rationally planned collectivities, with formal structures and explicit policies and rules governing significant segments of their behavior.

But rationality and formalism should not be overstressed since agencies are also social systems that adaptively respond to external and internal pressures, and that generate informal patterns that may both facilitate and hamper goal attainment. The dynamic interrelations among parts of an agency and between it and units in its environment cannot be fully understood by reference to formal arrangements, administrative provisions, and professed goals. The implementation of any technology and the introduction of new procedures generate and are shaped by forces that are partially beyond administrative control and rational planning.

Keeping these general perspectives in mind, several case examples involving socio-behavioral practice will first be reviewed. Points at which organizational issues are readily apparent in the reports of these developments will be noted, and an attempt will then be made to derive a series of organizational requisites essential for use of socio-behavioral technology.

---

[1] For a discussion of the distinctive characteristics of human service organizations, see Robert D. Vinter, "The Analysis of Treatment Organizations," *Social Work,* Vol. 8, No. 3 (July, 1963), pp. 2-15; and for an analysis of the qualities and practices of these organizations as they relate to differential outcomes, see Stanton Wheeler, "The Structure of Formally Organized Socialization Settings," in Orville Brim and Stanton Wheeler, *Socialization After Childhood* (New York: Wiley, 1966), pp. 51-107.

[2] For a discussion of approaches to organizational analysis, see Alvin Gouldner, "Organizational Analysis," in Robert Merton, Leonard Bloom, and Leonard Cottrell, eds., *Sociology Today* (New York: Basic Books, 1959), pp. 400-428; also see Amitai Etzioni, *Modern Organizations* (Englewood Cliffs, New Jersey: Prentice-Hall, 1964), pp. 20-50; and James Thompson, *Organizations in Action* (New York: McGraw-Hill, 1967).

CASE EXAMPLES

The first example to be considered is a report by Wetzel of behavioral treatment of a ten-year-old boy in a residential institution for children.[3] The boy was in and out of this institution and of courts, schools, and foster homes, for a period of more than five years for severe compulsive stealing, enuresis, tantrums, and other acting-out behavior. It is not necessary to present here the assessment and treatment protocol, but compulsive stealing and enuresis were the problematic behaviors selected, with the former receiving primary attention. This study was undertaken in a typical children's institution where opportunities for behavioral control were far from unlimited. The children lived in the institution but attended a community school during the day. Wetzel was particularly interested in evaluating what could be done in such a setting where the majority of staff were untrained cottage parents, recreation aides, cooks, and so forth. He was able to design and implement a treatment plan by which the problematic behaviors were eliminated within a three and one-half month period. An essential part of the plan involved the choice of one staff member who would function as an effective reinforcer. Reinforcement was then made contingent upon not stealing. The cook was selected as the reinforcing person, and she and other members of the staff were instructed in a specified set of procedures. Wetzel points out that the client was not anxious to change his behavior; in fact, there were intrinsic satisfactions and environmental contingencies that maintained the stealing. Therefore, the environment had to be re-ordered so that the stealing behavior was no longer gratifying.

A number of procedures were employed that involved organizational considerations. The staff had to be trained in behavior modification principles, in specific recording procedures, and in particular techniques for this case. Experience later showed that the content had to be communicated to staff frequently, and that pre-treatment training was insufficient.

Baseline performance data were required about the client's stealing behavior, visits with the cook, bedwetting, and so forth. Staff were often inconsistent in their recording and in controlling visits with the cook. This became particularly problematic as the plan started to become effective. Staff then modified their standards informally and inconsistently, necessitating close monitoring. The feasibility of monitoring and controlling staff behaviors is an important criterion against which to judge any behavior modification plan. For example, staff observed, and were concerned about other inappropriate behavior of this client and other clients in the unit.

There were many staff members in direct or indirect contact with the boy

---

[3] Ralph Wetzel, "Use of Behavioral Techniques in a Case of Compulsive Stealing," Peter J. Lang, "The Transfer of Treatment," and James A. Dinsmoor, "Comments on Wetzel's Treatment of a Case of Compulsive Stealing," all in *Journal of Consulting Psychology,* Vol. 30, No. 5 (October, 1966), pp. 367-380.

in this agency, greatly aggravating control problems. Three shifts of cottage staff were assigned each day and, in addition, the employment turnover rate was fairly high in this institution. As a result, mechanisms had to be developed for continual training and supervision of staff. Special communication procedures were needed between shifts of staff workers. Despite efforts to accomplish these plans, there continued to be inconsistencies that impinged on the client's treatment plan. Staff were helped to become aware of inconsistent behavior and to devise procedures for handling problematic situations. Guiding and controlling the behavior of staff groups, as well as individuals, then, involves a high level of coordinative effort to maintain the consistency required by this technology.

Generalization of non-stealing behavior to the boy's usual social environment posed a number of problems. Although his stealing stopped in the institution, the staff did not know whether it would reappear in other social settings, except in the school attended while he was in the institution. Opportunities for observations outside the institution, at home, and in other social situations needed to be provided. Positive reinforcement of non-stealing behavior after departure from the institution seems essential to maintain the modifications achieved within the program.

The Wetzel report reveals several organizational requisites that must be satisfied and indicates that a socio-behavioral technology can be implemented even in an on-going institutional program. It also suggests a number of areas that could have been planned more carefully to achieve greater environmental control.

Our second case example illustrates the application of socio-behavioral theory, and particularly of operant procedures, in a cottage at the National Training School for Boys in Washington, D. C.[4] The CASE II project was initiated by Harold Cohen and his colleagues to stimulate the educational achievement of delinquent boys and to evaluate the utility of operant procedures with this type of clientele. Originally, the project was entirely focused on education and spanned only a three-hour period each day. Recently, it was extended to a 24-hour program for a cottage of 28 boys, representative of all youth in the institution.

Cohen utilizes a system of external reinforcers (points that are earned and exchanged only by the earner for money or services) and has tried to simulate a "real-world" economy to improve academic, vocational, and social behavior. This project is especially noteworthy in the socio-behavioral literature because of its attempts to link the institutional program directly to the future social environment of the clients. In addition, the behavior upon which the

---

[4] Harold Cohen, James A. Filipiczak, and John S. Bis, "Contingencies Applicable to Special Education of Delinquents: Establishing 24-hour Control in an Experimental Cottage" (Silver Springs, Maryland: Institute for Behavioral Research, Inc., 1966, mimeographed).

points are contingent is that which may be objectively measured with reference to modification goals; examples are test scores, completion of programmed courses; and demonstrated ability to work for specified periods of time. An elaborate design has been developed for both the formal and the informal program of the cottage. This project has been under way for only a short period, but preliminary results show very positive outcomes with reference to institutional and post-institutional behavior. Anti-social behavior within the cottage is reported to be almost non-existent, and behavior, such as truancy, is less than half the rate for the rest of the institution.

The CASE II project report makes clear that many aspects of organizational behavior must be controlled for an effective behavior modification program. In order to implement the regimen, the physical and social environment had to be explicitly designed in a manner and with equipment different from that found in the usual training school for delinquent boys. The education program, for example, included 89 programmed or auto-instructional courses, each of which had particular resource requirements in materials and staff. Socio-behavioral technology, like any other treatment approach, poses its own requirements for essential artifacts, material and even architecture. The agency must be able to supply these and to make the re-arrangements required by the plan.

Introduction of a token economy throughout the cottage (work, leisure, education, cottage living were all included) required considerable ingenuity and innovation in organizational arrangements. Special provisions were required for private study, for availability of facilities throughout the day and evening, and for accurate and consistent monitoring. Choices had to be made about which behavior was to be controlled under the point system, since it was not feasible to include every possible activity. Cohen deliberately chose activities that were linked most directly to the extra-institutional environment such as education, work, and parole status.

Professional and non-professional staff had to be trained in the use of the behavior modification procedures. CASE II used many non-professional staff who had been in the institution for a number of years. It was found that they could be successfully retrained, but ingenuity was important in the conduct of this in-service training. The project is now being engineered for the total institution. Cohen and his staff have observed that variables such as size and organizational complexity require particular consideration, because preconditions sufficient for one cottage or unit may be inadequate when implemented for the entire organization.

A third example is the Hartwig project described by Rose earlier in this volume.[5] The organizational features of this effort will be examined without

---

[5] Sheldon Rose, "A Behavioral Approach to Group Treatment of Children," pp. 39-55.

restating its details. The Hartwig project differs from those reported by Cohen and Wetzel, because it was developed in an open community-based agency rather than in a closed institution. Because of this, variations can be expected in the organizational requisites. Rose's account of the Hartwig project touches on several requisites. First of all, means had to be developed for routinized assessment and referral of potential clients by such referring agents as teachers, and staff of the police youth bureau. Instruments were needed to present information about who defined the unacceptable behavior, about conditions preceding and accompanying this behavior, as well as about the environmental consequences of the behavior. Next, baseline performance criteria were necessary for each client, and in the case of group treatment approaches, for behavior at the group as well as at the individual level. Information had to be obtained from school teachers, parents, and staff members in other agencies. It was observed that other agencies had different goals and employed contrasting technologies. Thus, it was difficult to obtain sufficient comparable information unless some controls were instituted.

Mechanisms for monitoring behavior pose additional requirements once the baseline criteria have been established. Rose noted that workers' observations were inadequate for this purpose and that systematic procedures had to be developed for monitoring intra-group and extra-group behavior. The school and the home were chosen in this project as the sites for periodic monitoring, and precise information from these sources was required at particular points.

It was reported that frequent problems were encountered in the development of systematic assessment and reporting procedures. Information had to be obtained in brief periods of time and had to be analyzed continuously so that the findings could be used in modifying or stabilizing treatment plans. Attention also was directed to procedures of "feed-back" to teachers and parents so that the information communicated would have the desired effect rather than an unanticipated and undesirable consequence.

Staff without professional training were employed in the Hartwig project, and like Wetzel, Rose found that they could be successfully trained in the use of socio-behavioral theory. In fact, Rose implies that non-professionals may be trained to implement much of the direct service to clients, with professional staff responsible for design and overall supervision of the program.[6]

---

[6] Albert Bandura and Richard Walters, *Social Learning and Personality Development* (New York: Holt, Rinehart and Winston, 1963), pp. 224-259. They also suggest similar roles for professionally trained staff.

DISCUSSION OF REQUISITES

The three reports illustrate a number of important organizational requisites for effective use of a socio-behavioral technology.[7] Let us restate the issues derived from examination of these cases and consider their more general implications. Attention will be focused on the distinctive requirements posed by the use of socio-behavioral technologies and on those requirements that are essential for goal attainment and survival of viable human service organizations. Inevitably, the examination of prerequisites will be incomplete and tentative, and the discussion of rationale for choice of certain preconditions rather than others will not be completely specific. The utilization of socio-behavioral practice in these organizations is very new; much more research and extensive application under variable conditions is necessary before prerequisites can be unambiguously specified.

Information Requirements

The information requirements of this technology are far more demanding in several areas than those of other treatment approaches. Concrete and specific information about client malperformance must be obtained from problem-defining agents outside the agency (e.g., referral sources) as well as within. In the absence of this knowledge, it is impossible to formulate behavior modification objectives and to note changes. Procedures for obtaining baseline performance data for individual clients and groups of clients must be organizationally routinized, as both the Wetzel and Rose reports indicate. Some work has been done in this area and preliminary findings indicate that procedures can be successfully operationalized and engineered.[8] These results also suggest that instruments and procedures can be established not only for practitioners in their programming for clients but also for agency administrators who need systematic information for planning and evaluative purposes.

When change procedures have been initiated, additional types of information are needed on a continuing basis. There must be observational assessment

---

[7] It was not possible to identify in this paper the organizational precondition for the example of casework treatment reported by Richard Stuart. His attention was directed primarily to client-worker interaction and only indirectly to the agency. There is no reason to believe, however, that the preconditions identified in this paper would not be equally applicable in casework treatment.

[8] For a discussion of one approach in the development of systematic recording procedures in a social agency, see James Seaberg, "Case Recording by Code," *Social Work,* Vol. 10, No. 1 (October, 1965), pp. 92-99. Also see Robert D. Vinter, Rosemary C. Sarri, Darrel Vorwaller, and Walter E. Schafer, *Pupil Behavior Inventory* (Ann Arbor: Campus Publishers, 1966); Edgar F. Borgatta and David Fanshel, *Behavioral Characteristics of Children* (New York: Child Welfare League of America, 1965); Eugene Litwak, et al. "A Design of Utilization of Special Services in Detroit Public Schools," (Ann Arbor: The University of Michigan, 1965, unpublished manuscript).

and feedback of information about client behavior relevant to the foci of treatment. The availability today of automated information systems makes it possible to plan for rapid feedback of needed information to the appropriate staff. The application of these systems in most social agencies, however, will require substantial changes in information collection and processing.

Staff activities must be monitored in order to maintain adherence to the modification program and consistency among personnel. There must be continuing ways to determine the degree to which changed behavior is sustained in diverse situations during and subsequent to the modification program. Far too often, today, practitioners rely on highly impressionistic information, directly contrary to the requirements of a socio-behavioral technology. Taken together, these demands call for markedly improved systems for the collection, analysis, and feedback of specific kinds of information throughout the agency. The Wetzel and Cohen cases document the problems of fulfilling these requirements in the context of multi-staff institutional programs, while the Rose case points to the problems of crossing agency boundaries in obtaining information essential to the technology.

Staff Selection and Training

The introduction of a socio-behavioral technology is likely to require new staff or, at least, the retraining of existing personnel. Both professional staff and other echelons will be affected by the different performance requirements. The case examples all illustrate that non-professional staff can be trained to apply successfully behavior modification procedures. In each situation, explicit instruction was necessary and, furthermore, continuing training was required because of staff turnover and tendencies to drift back to former practices.

Coordination and Control

Much more than in-service training is required to implement a socio-behavioral technology. Conduct of each modification program calls for re-specification of responsibilities among certain staff members, and, equally important, for arrangements to articulate the behaviors of all others in a unified, consistent plan of service. Authority and control structures in agencies must insure the performance of the required behavior by all members and yet not provoke responses of resistance or apathy. Existing authority structures in many social agencies permit bifurcation in the management and treatment of clients, with the frequent outcome that rehabilitative goals are displaced by custodial or managerial goals.[9] Management and treatment functions must be

---

[9] David Street, Robert D. Vintner and Charles Perrow, *Organization for Treatment* (New York: Free Press Division of Macmillan, 1966), pp. 93-137.

integrated as these impinge on the client(s). Engineering problems are often enormous, particularly in the large complex agencies that provide twenty-four-hour care for clients—prisons, hospitals, nursing homes, and so forth. The utilization of socio-behavioral technologies will not prevent bifurcation or goal displacement. Therefore, special procedures must be instituted. For example, closed institutions may utilize an approach in which treatment is decentralized and integrated with management tasks at the living unit level.

Agencies in which there are large numbers of staff who represent different professions may have additional problems of coordination, because each of these groups may resist bureaucratic controls. Some mechanisms have been developed whereby the basis and criteria for allocating authority complement professional roles and structures, and still meet technical requirements for control. Goss has described a number of mechanisms employed in general hospitals whereby certain areas of physicians' roles are controlled by formal bureaucratic mechanisms and, in other areas, high degrees of informality and individual autonomy are allowed to prevail.[10]

Relatively high levels of specialization in staff roles can be expected if widely varied socio-behavioral technologies are utilized to attain the desired change goals for clients. Here, again, decentralization of decision-making about treatment planning and implementation is one strategy for resolution of control problems. However, this may be insufficient if a client is exposed to several different and, perhaps, unrelated technologies in different departments of the agency.

The importance of coordination is obvious if rational organizational behavior is to be enhanced. Nonetheless, as was pointed out earlier, the agency is also to be viewed as a social system that adaptively responds to external and internal pressures. These pressures may generate informal patterns that may hamper treatment objectives, and yet they are often ignored when considering coordinative mechanisms. If socio-behavioral technologies are to be successfully employed, social system requirements must be served. The Essexfield project, described by Thomas, is an example of an attempt to create a new type of social system within the agency as the primary treatment strategy.[11] To serve these requirements minimally, the agency would need to provide mechanisms for coping with or responding to informal client systems behavior, unanticipated consequences, or side effects of rationally planned interventions.

---

[10] Mary Goss, "Patterns of Bureaucracy Among Hospital Staff Physicians," in Eliot Friedson, ed., *The Hospital in Modern Society* (New York: Free Press Division of Macmillan, 1963), pp. 170-194.

[11] Edwin J. Thomas, "The Socio-Behavioral Approach: Illustrations and Analysis," pp. 4-5, 8ff.

Redesign of Agency Environments

Introduction of new technologies based on socio-behavioral theory is likely to call for extensive alterations in the design of services, and, not infrequently, of physical facilities. It poses its own requirements for essential artifacts, material, and even, perhaps, architecture. The need for such changes in the examples given here was more apparent in the CASE II project that centered on a complete residential unit. Considerable effort and imagination went into the design of new types of "hardware," particularly in the educational program. Greater use of electronic and physical hardware, heretofore mainly nonexistent in social agencies, can be safely predicted. There are obvious parallels in the new developments that are taking place today in education where computers, electronic consoles, and teaching machines are increasingly employed.

Much more than alterations are involved in the technical or service arrangements directly relevant to a behavior modification program. The case examples given point to the manifold ways in which a broad range of physical and social agency patterns serve as controlling conditions and reinforcing contingencies (positive and negative) with respect to behavior modification programs. These reinforcing contingencies must be assessed and utilized planfully if socio-behavioral approaches are to be employed successfully. Many social agencies today provide extensive physical and social deprivations and punishments, and very few gratifications.[12] In assessing positive and negative reinforcers in the agency, attention is to be given to individual, group, and community variations in perceptions of what is or may be reinforcing or punishing. Having accomplished this, a balanced economy of gratifications must be provided and controlled, with mechanisms for allocations of rewards throughout the system by clients as well as staff. The findings from studies of the systems for distribution of rewards and sanctions in human service organization provide additional specification of these requirements.[13]

New models for closed institutions will clearly be required if simulation of crucial features of the external environment is to be achieved, as required by many behavior modification procedures. The Wetzel and Cohen reports both deal with the redesign of aspects of the agency environment, and there are other extensive plans reported in the literature.[14] Blum and Polansky, for

---

[12] For penetrating descriptions of these conditions in human service organizations, see Erving Goffman, "On the Characteristics of Total Institutions: The Inmate World and Staff-Inmate Relations," in Donald Cressey, ed., *The Prison: Studies in Institutional Organization and Change* (New York: Holt, Rinehart, and Winston, 1961), pp. 15-106; Lloyd M. McKorkle and Richard Korn, "Resocialization Within the Walls," *The Annals,* 293 (May, 1954), pp. 88-98; Julius Roth, *Timetables* (Indianapolis: Bobbs-Merrill, 1963); and Brim and Wheeler, *op. cit.,* pp. 83-89.

[13] See Street et al., *op cit.,* pp. 224-227 and 279-285.

[14] Teodoro Ayllon and Nicholas H. Azrin, "The Measurement and Reinforcement of Behavior of Psychotics," *Journal of the Experimental Analysis of Behavior,* Vol. 8, No. 6 (November, 1965), pp. 357-385; Teodoro Ayllon and Jack Michael, "The Psychi-

example, observed that the organizational structure of staff roles played a significant part in children's behavior patterns in a residential setting.[15] Worker interactions with clients were governed more by the organizational structure than by individual attributes. In community agencies, such as that in which the Hartwig project is located, services are provided outside the usual building-centered program and the eight-to-five office schedule. This requires modification of many contemporary agency arrangements if provision is to be made for continuing innovation, adaptation, and flexibility. Some agencies have been able to implement programs of this type, but problems and strains inevitably emerge unless agencies provide mechanisms for routinized problem-solving to handle the continuing need for adaptation and change. Routinized problem-solving procedures will also stimulate staff to conceptualize more alternatives to existing operational patterns and to predict probable consequences from alternative courses of action. Thus, forecasting and planning for the future will be enhanced. Discussion earlier in the paper about informational requirements is also pertinent here since rationalized problem-solving by all levels of staff require the feed-back of information about cases and case management, about programs, and about outcomes.[16] Despite the difficulties, identification and deliberate control or redesign of intra-agency environments is necessary in order not to negate behavioral treatment plans.

External Linkages

Important connections between intra-agency procedures and external processes were cited at several points in the prior case examples and discussion. These involved (1) the obtaining of client malperformance information and definitions from outside sources, (2) the establishment of behavior modification criteria having direct relevance to conventional roles and standards, (3) the creation of intra-mural situations and experiences directly analogous to externally significant behavioral areas, and (4) the problem of sustaining behavioral change through reinforcement procedures and monitoring performance after departure from the agency. The first three of these are essential to insure that treatment plans focus directly on behavioral patterns at issue in

atric Nurse as a Behavioral Engineer," in Arthur Staats, ed., *Human Learning* (New York: Holt, Rinehart and Winston, 1964), pp. 445-448; Sidney Bijou, "Experimental Studies of Child Behavior, Normal and Deviant," in Leonard Krasner and Leonard Ullmann, eds., *Research in Behavior Modification* (New York: Holt, Rinehart and Winston, 1965), pp. 56-82.

[15] Arthur Blum and Norman A. Polansky, "Effect of Staff Role on Children's Verbal Accessibility," *Social Work*, Vol. 6, No. 1 (January, 1961), pp. 29-34.

[16] John K. Harris has suggested that administrative planning and decision-making would be markedly enhanced by the use of more systematic information processing. See John K. Harris, "System Designs for Welfare Programs: The Role of EDP," *Public Welfare*, Vol. 24, No. 2 (April, 1966), pp. 112-117.

the client's "real world" environment, while the fourth addresses generalization of changes into post-treatment situations. Also implicated is the notion that the client's experience is appropriately viewed as a career into, through, and out of the agency. This perspective requires that continuing attention be directed to the linkages between the external environment and intra-agency phenomena.[17] All of these requisites appear more difficult to fulfill where client populations are abstracted from their usual social contexts and where the internal agency environment is markedly different from conventional contexts.[18] The spanning or surmounting of agency boundaries is a special problem where it becomes necessary to effect controls on the client's external social system. Where the target of change is a group or neighborhood rather than individual clients, still other approaches may be required to cope with environmental linkages. Some strategies of the latter type were suggested in the paper that considered application of socio-behavioral theory to community practice.[19] Unless effective external linkages are developed, behavioral modification programs risk being irrelevant as well as impotent.

CONCLUSIONS

This analysis of the organizational requisites clearly indicates that a number of essentials can be identified. Furthermore, preliminary evidence suggests that many of these can be met at least partially. Introduction of this technology can be expected to have both direct and indirect benefits for social agencies. At the interpersonal and community levels of intervention, problems have frequently arisen in the past because external forces exerted considerable pressure on human service organizations to concretize and specify both goals and means. The latter task was particularly difficult because of the ambiguity and indeterminancy of many human relations technologies. Socio-behavioral theory provides a marked contrast to theories that underlie many of these other interpersonal change technologies. It is based on empirically validated knowledge and is specific, prescriptive and adaptable. It also demands that linkages be established between the problematic behavior that brought the client to the agency, treatment plans and outcomes, and agency goals. Far greater attention is paid to the design and engineering of service technologies directly related to behavior desired in the larger social system. What distinguishes the socio-

---

[17] Eugene Litwak and Henry J. Meyer, "A Balance Theory of Coordination Between Organizations and Community Primary Groups," *Administrative Science Quarterly,* Vol. 11, No. 1 (June, 1966), pp. 31-58.

[18] Robert Rapaport, *The Community as Doctor* (Springfield, Illinois: C. C. Thomas and Co., 1960).

[19] Philip A. Fellin, Jack Rothman and Henry J. Meyer, "Implications of Socio-Behavioral Theory for Community Organization Practice," pp. 119-135.

behavioral technology is the extent to which its particular requirements are explicit through and integral to its procedures, rather than suggested by its ideology or action orientations.

For the agency, utilization of this approach is potentially valuable, because its behaviorally specific objectives and prescriptions for action facilitate comparisons across levels, subsystems, and organizations. The focus on specificity of change goals is congruent with the need to achieve greater demonstrability of service effectiveness. Rising pressures are being exerted today on social agencies to specify their goals and validate their accomplishments.

Although limits on rationality are recognized, a socio-behavioral approach suggests that the agency can be conceived as an instrument for behavior modification at individual, group and larger social system levels. It is, perhaps, too early to determine if there are unique requirements posed by the utilization of this technology. There is little doubt that as the tenets of this technology are accepted and its procedures introduced in a broader range of organizations, marked changes can be expected in the physical and social design of agencies, in the deployment of staff, in procedures for information collection and processing, in mechanisms for monitoring staff and client behavior and evaluating outcomes, and in the explicit linking of treatment technologies to clients' usual social environments.

Discussion

Question 1. I am not clear about whether the client or the group with which you are working is "let in" on the strategy of this approach. To what extent do you make explicit what you are doing, why you are doing it, and what the outcome is that you anticipate or hope for? Or, is this something which clients or groups simply experience? Are they sort of passive recipients? To what extent are they "in on the game" with you?

Sarri. One of the things we proposed at the organizational level involved having clients participate in decision making. There are a number of ways, for example, in which the Cohen experiment at the National Training School for Boys has creatively involved delinquent boys in crucial decision making about the design and implementation of the educational and living program.

Thomas. This morning, the papers by Stuart and Rose very strongly emphasized that in the situations in which you have voluntary relationships, everything is aboveboard and explicitly understood. Both Stuart and Rose emphasized this very strongly, perhaps even more strongly than some of the rest of us might. However, there is a behavioral question here. Leaving ethics aside, there is a simple matter of efficiency involved. It is really an old question and not particular to socio-behavioral theory. Under some circumstances, awareness of the conditions of change may retard progress whereas in other cases, such awareness may facilitate change. Recent research gives indication of some, but not very many, of the conditions under which client awareness of the contingencies and of the controlling conditions will bring about greater as opposed to lesser movement toward the treatment objectives.

Now, for the matter of ethics. Some people have alleged that there is something Machiavellian and terribly manipulative about the socio-behavioral approach. This is incorrect. The problems involving ethics are the same ones we always have had. We have always had to decide whether what we do on behalf of clients is consistent with the ethics of our profession and the values of society. The socio-behavioral approach is a body of knowledge and mode of practice to be employed to attain ethically suitable objectives.